TALK DIRTY
ITALIAN

D0207796

BEYOND CAZZO: THE CURSES, SLANG, AND STREET LINGO YOU NEED TO KNOW WHEN YOU SPEAK ITALIANO

TALK DIRTY

ITALIAN

ALEXIS MUNIER & EMMANUEL TICHELLI

Avon, Massachusetts

Published by
Adams Media, a division of F+W Media, Inc.
57 Littlefield Street, Avon, MA 02322
www.adamsmedia.com

ISBN 13: 978-1-59869-769-8
ISBN 10: 1-59869-769-2

Printed in the United States of America.

J I H G F E D C B

Library of Congress Cataloging-in-Publication Data
is available from the publisher.

This publication is designed to provide accurate and authoritative information with regard to the subject matter covered. It is sold with the understanding that the publisher is not engaged in rendering legal, accounting, or
other professional advice. If legal advice or other expert assistance is requi-
red, the services of a competent professional person should be sought.
   —From a *Declaration of Principles* jointly adopted by a Committee of the
American Bar Association and a Committee of Publishers and Associations

Many of the designations used by manufacturers and sellers to distinguish
their product are claimed as trademarks. Where those designations appear
in this book and Adams Media was aware of a trademark claim, the designations have been printed with initial capital letters.

Interior illustrations ©iStockphoto.com/Matt Knannlein.

This book is available at quantity discounts for bulk purchases.
For information, please call 1-800-289-0963.

CONTENTS

ITALIAN
READER
ADVISORY

To my nonna Angela,
whose kindness, wisdom, and faith always
prevented her from using *Dirty Italian*
even when she should have.
Emmanuel Tichelli

To my Papa Colonel,
who hates pasta, loves spaghetti westerns,
and still calls them "Eye-talians."
Alexis Munier

DISCLAIMER

All entries come with sample sentences as well

as common use and literal translations with the

exception of the dirtiest of the dirty.

You'll know them by

XXX: Too Dirty to Translate.

INTRODUCTION

What's the point of speaking Italian slang? Why, to understand what the Italians are actually saying, of course! Movies from *cinecittà*, the Italian Hollywood, lyrics of a song, lines of a contemporary author, or programs *della tivù spazzatura* are all made specifically for Italians. While your schoolbook Italian is a good base, without slang you'll miss the beauty of Bertolucci's films, Bocelli's vocals, and Benigni's humor.

Rather than parade around Rome with a cheesy phrasebook for common conversations, you are better off with a copy of *Talk Dirty: Italian*. After all, would you rather bring home the usual souvenirs or the person who sold them to you? We can't claim this book will do the latter, but without it you're almost certain to leave *la bella Italia* with an awful plastic Leaning Tower of Pisa. Remember, Italy is not France: attempting to speak the real day-to-day language of Italians will win you big bonus points and impress everyone you meet. While they may laugh at your mistakes, they'll appreciate your bravado, for which you will certainly be rewarded.

Acknowledgments

A heartfelt thank-you to Mara Cavadini, our reference Italian teacher who, despite a baby in diapers, found the time to get down and dirty for us.

Big thanks to Daniele and Stefania Basilico, Massimo Palo, Marco Lorio, the Vanuccis, and the Tichellis, who all helped enormously in writing this book.

Special thanks to Domenico Mariani, Erminia Lorio, Giancarlo Ramazzini, as well as the inhabitants of *il piccolo mondo antico di Fogazzaro* who unknowingly inspired this book with their infamous interjections and slang.

And one last thanks to our publisher Adams Media and its supportive team, including Paula Munier, Sara Stock, and Katrina Schroeder.

CHAPTER ONE

Qui non si parla italiano:

What's That Strange Language?

The United States of Italy, Regionalism, and Foreign Influences

Despite its long history, Italy is more insolent teenager than old fogey. In fact, until 1870, there was no proper *Italia*, just a patchwork of *ducati* "dukedoms," kingdoms (often held by other empires), small republics, and *stati pontifici* "lands held by the Catholic Church." There were separate dialects and peoples like Lombards, Venetians, Romans, and Neapolitans . . . but no Italians. Italy's creation began with the unusual union of the kingdom of Sardegna's army and the Republican army led by Giuseppe Garibaldi. On the way to unify Northern and Southern Italy, territories belonging to the Church that cut *lo stivale*, "the boot," in two, had to be conquered. *I due mondi* were reunified when the Italian army entered Rome and made it Italy's *capitale*.

The next step involved creating the notion of Italian identity among a patchwork of diverse dialects and cultures. Before independence, much of the country had been ruled by *potenze stranieri*, "foreign powers," who left their distinctive cultural and linguistic marks on these occupied territories. You'll find Albanian, Greek, French, and North African words in the southern dialects, and German and French in the northern ones. As a result, there wasn't *una lingua italiana* but *diversi italiani.* To remedy this, *l'italiano pulito*, "clean Italian," was the goal of the state. One dialect in particular was promoted above all others, *il fiorentino*. This Tuscan dialect was considered the purest and least contaminated. Publications, education, communication, and arts now had to be written or spoken in this new standard Italian. Dialects were considered *sporchi*, "dirty," and their use was banned.

As you can imagine, people were not especially keen to drop their native dialects. While standard or textbook Italian is now used on official documents, at school, on TV, and in most publications, you'll certainly hear *l'italiano sporco*, "dirty Italian," while traveling and you will face some difficulty understanding a simple day-to-day conversation. Dialects never disappeared completely and remain the closest language to people's feelings and emotions. You'll find some important or frequent regional expressions in this book to help you along; they'll be marked with their origin in parentheses, e.g., "(Roma)."

Origin of Italian Slang

Criminality and Secret Codes

The underworld creates its own slang words to separate itself from the general population and to keep its evil deeds under wraps. *Furbo*, slang for "thief," has now transitioned into regular Italian. The meaning has changed, though, and *furbo* now refers to a clever person or smartass. So you can see the ingrained respect and admiration Italians have (despite their protests) for criminal activity.

Criminal slang, *il gergo criminale,* was once only comprehensible to the Mob. Words like *Cosa nostra, Camora, padrino,* and *omertà* meant nothing to the uninitiated. Times have changed, and they're now understood by all Italians. Once this criminal slang becomes commonplace, the Mob must invent new slang to keep their activities secret. Even the godfather Toto Rino, hidden in the Sicilian country-side for years, managed to keep contact with his collaborators using a system of codes and a bible. Mobsters who wind up in jail are still in touch with the exterior without the authorities even noticing.

Coke Land

The forbidden world is a big user and creator of slang. Initially reserved for junkies and dealers, these words are now popular with all Italians. Among them you'll find deformations of English words, although much of the time their literal meaning has changed. Words used when someone is high now apply to express the effects of drinking, astonishment, or mental health.

Ma ti buchi?
Are you out of your mind?
Lit. Do you take shots?

È partito.
He's drunk/high.

Quest'idea mi fa troppo tripare.
That idea is so trippy.

Sto allucinando.
I'm astonished.
Lit. I'm having hallucinations.

3

Youth Input

To speak dirty is similar to dressing differently from the mainstream: it's an act of revolt against the establishment, parents, and education. Creativity fuels slang and neologisms and new words are created every day. Some will pass through the social filter, some will pass directly into standard Italian, and most will fail immediately.

Internet, Nerds, and Video Games

Information technology has introduced many English terms in Italian. There's no point to writing them as you already know them. Just keep in mind that regular verbs end with the *-are* suffix, which is used to Italianize the English verbs. The IT terms will build a bridge between you and the Italians you're trying to converse with. Okay, you may look like a geek, but remember that nowadays geeks have talents that macho guys don't have, and the computer skills that the modern society appreciates and rewards.

chattare
to chat

s.m.s.are
to send an S.M.S

downloadare
to download

Size Matters

Regular words are often too long and not hip enough. Below find two ways to shorten them, with the apostrophe marking the cut. From now on we'll use the following abbreviations: **TBI** for the textbook Italian you probably already know and **DI** for Dirty Italian, which will put you "in the know."

4

Cut the beginning

TBI   questo, questa
DI   'sto, 'sta
this

Cut the end

TBI   ragazzi, mpl
DI   raga'
guys

TBI   bellezza, f
DI   bellé'
beauty

Verbs are usually shortened and written without their final *e* when the next word starts with a vowel.

TBI   **Non ho voglia di andare al mare.**
DI   **Non ho voglia d'andar al mare.**
I don't want to go to the sea.

Too Short!

Some Italian chauvinist pigs claim a short word is like a shorthaired woman: it could look much sexier or trendier with some extensions. You already have the base; let us provide you with the suffixes. You may spend more time pronouncing the words, but when you master this art you'll sound more like a native.

-accio, -accia

This suffix gives a dirty or negative vibe to the word.

TBI   ragazzo, m
DI   ragazzaccio, m

guy, dude

TBI **Lorenzo**
DI **Lorenzaccio**
Laurence

-uccio, -uccia

This suffix is employed as a *vezzeggiativo*, "diminutive," which makes a word "cuter."

TBI **tesoro, m**
DI **tesoruccio, m**
treasure, sweetie

TBI **amore, m**
DI **amoruccio, m**
love

-etto, -etta and *-ino, -ina*

Suffixes used to make something smaller or of less importance.

TBI **nonna, f**
DI **nonnetta, f**
grandma

TBI **figa, f**
DI **fighetta, f**
chick, lit. little pussy

-one, -ona

This suffix inflates the word, and makes the object bigger or more important.

TBI **successo, m,**
DI **successone, m**
success, lit. big success

TBI   ladro, ladra
DI   ladrone, ladrona
thief, lit. big thief

-uncolo, -uncola
This suffix is a pure slang invention meaning strange or bad.

TBI   ladro, ladra
DI   ladruncolo, ladruncola
thief, lit. bad thief

Too Much!
No matter where in the world you go, exaggeration is a teenage must. Italians rely on excessive behaviors, attitudes, and over-emphasis. For the equivalent of a free facelift, instead of the traditional *molto*, "very," use *troppo*, "too much."

TBI   La festa è un vero successo/La festa è veramente
        un successo
DI   La festa è troppo un successo!
The party is a big hit! lit. The party is too much a success!

The prefixes *arci-*, *mega-*, *super-* and the suffix *-issimo*, *-issima* all mean *molto*, "very" or "a lot," depending on the stem they attach to. Despite the choice of different superlatives, Italian teens mostly use the *-issimo* ending.

TBI   Sono molto stanco.
DI   Sono superstanco.
I'm exhausted.

TBI   Sei molto bravo.
DI   Sei bravissimo.
You're great.

TBI   Hai comprato una casa molta bella.
DI   Hai comprato una casa megabella.
You bought a mega-beautiful house.

Scusate My Italian

The textbook Italian you first learned may seem uptight or boring when compared to the language used by the average Joe, *l'Italiano medio*. Some mistakes in Italian are indeed acceptable in Dirty Italian. What's important is the message, not its traditional form—so make mistakes too and you'll sound like a native!

Incorrect Verb Tenses

If you struggled with the choice of verb tense in indirect speech, *Talk Dirty. Italian* will ease your worries. In **TBI** reported speech uses one of the past tenses, but in **DI** reported speech uses the same tense that the original speech used.

Direct speech:
Mi ha detto: "Ti amo."
She told me: "I love you."

Reported speech:
TBI   **Mi ha detto che mi amava.**
She told me she loved me.

Reported speech:
DI   **Mi ha detto che mi ama.**
She told me she loves me.

Useless Repetitions

What's the point of saying something twice? What's the point of saying something twice? Repetition is a common error you hear in spoken Italian, so common that it sounds almost right. Redundancies happen mostly with verb complements, including pronouns, and direct and indirect objects.

TBI   **Ho detto a tua sorella di stare attenta.**
DI   **Glielo ho detto a tua sorella di stare attenta.**
I told your sister to watch out.
Lit. I told her—your sister—to watch out.

TBI   **Mi piace la cioccolata.**
DI   **A me, mi piace la cioccolata.**
I like chocolate.
Lit. To me the chocolate pleases me.

Conclusion

This chapter is not exhaustive, but it provides some basic information on forming Italian slang. Don't worry if you have no clue what half the words in this book mean. Use your months or years of studying Italian as a base, and use *Talk Dirty: Italian* to go from clueless tourist to savvy traveler. Remember though, the key to mastering any language is immersion. If you can't spend your summers in Italy, at least head down to the closest authentic Italian restaurant and try out your skills.

CHAPTER TWO

Ciao bambino:

Getting Off on the Right Foot

While Italy has a reputation of adoring little ones, you won't see many of them playing *sulla piazza del paese* anymore. Couples used to have *tanti bambini*, and the wife usually stayed home and took care of them while the husband went off to work. One reason behind this could be that *il cattolicesimo* was strong nationwide and so was the power of Vatican City on the Italian government. As a result, *il divorzio* and *l'aborto* were denied. Nowadays, both women and men have to work to pay off their increasing credits and debts. As a modern nation, Italy has new idols: credit cards and consumption. The latest electronic equipment, fancy clothes, and expensive cars, along with access to contraceptives, have changed the face of Italy. Demanding jobs, less free time, and little household help have contributed to the Italian birth rate becoming one of the lowest in Europe. At only 1.2 children per woman, Italy is on par with many depressed former Soviet-block nations that now see children as a hindrance, not a *benedizione*. *Gli incentivi alla natalità* proposed by the second Berlusconi government, such as a 1,000 euro bonus for each child after the first, have not helped the situation.

If women have shown they can enter the workforce, men have shown that they can't do their part of the household chores. As children, teenagers, and young adults, most men were spoiled by their *mamme* until they got married. Remember, even nowadays, most men live with their parents up until marriage, which usually takes place in a man's early thirties. Once out of the nest, most of these men are still not ready to help their wives, preferring to hold out hope that one day their wives will become their *mamme*.

Meeting the Family and Friends

guaglione, guagliona (Napoletano)
man, lady, lit. boy, girl
Eh, guaglione, cosa vuoi da me?
Hey man, what do you want from me?

tipo, tipa
guy, girl, girlfriend, lit. type
Lasciate le tipe a casa. Sarà un weekend tra soli uomini.
Leave the girlfriends at home. It'll be a guys' weekend.

tizio, tizia,
guy, girl
Quel tizio non mi piace affatto.
I really don't like that guy.

ragazzaccio, m
bad boy

Sei un ragazzaccio: hai calpestato tutti i miei fiori.
You're a bad boy: you stepped on all my flowers.

zio, m
dude, lit. abbr. of *tizio*
Eh zio vieni qua un attimo!
Hey dude, come here for a minute!

bimbo, bimba
kid, abbr. of *bambino*, child
La mia bimba sapeva leggere a tre anni.
My kid could read at three years old.

pupo, pupa
kid, abbr. of *pupazzo*, puppet, *pupa* is also chick
Che bella pupa!
What a cute kid!

marmocchio, m
kid, brat; from the French *marmot*, brat
Quanto odio i marmocchi di mia sorella.
I can't stand my sister's brats.

diavoletto, m
kid, little devil
Ho incontrato Maya il suo diavoletto per strada.
I ran into Maya and her little devil on the street.

babbo, m (Tuscany)
daddy
Il mio babbo lavora anche di domenica.
My daddy also works on Sundays.

mamma, mammina, f
mom, mommy, lit. little mom

Dov'è la tua mammina, dolcezza?
Where's your mommy, sweetie?

supermamma, f
supermom
Lavora e cresce tre figli da sola—che supermamma.
She works and is raising three sons all by herself—what a supermom.

i miei/tuoi/suoi
my/your/his/her folks, lit. my/your/his/her
Vieni a casa mia, i miei non ci sono.
Come to my house, my folks aren't there.

fratellino/fratellone, m
little/big brother
Se vedo quel cretino del tuo fratellino lo prendo a schiaffi!
If I see your brother I'll slap him in the face.

sorellina/sorellona, f
little/big sister
Fausto e la sua sorellina non si somigliano per niente.
Fausto's little sister doesn't look anything like him.

fratellastro, m/sorellastra, f
stepbrother/stepsister, lit. bad brother/sister
La sorellastra di Davide mi piace un pacco.
I really like David's stepsister.

nonnino, nonnina
grandpa, grandma, lit. little grandfather/grandmother
Alessio sente molto la mancanza della sua nonnina.
Alessio really feels the loss of his grandma.

vecchiardo, vecchiarda
old fogey/bag, lit. bad old one
Non mi piace la vecchiarda che vive accanto a me.
I don't like the old bag who lives near me.

vecchietto, vecchietta
old person, lit. little old one
I vecchietti del quinto piano sono molto gentili.
The old people from the fifth floor are very nice.

Qualities and Quantities

del cazzo/menga (and other regional synonyms)
shitty, lit. of the dick
Non sopporto più questo paese del cazzo.
I can't stand this shitty country anymore.

If you think del cazzo *is too strong, then use one of the following:* da quattro soldi, *"of four coins," or* da strapazzo, *"of huge effort." Contrary to English, Italian reverses the strength of the expressions "f**king" and "shitty."* Del cazzo *is best translated into English as "shitty," while* di merda, *literally "shitty," is actually closer in vulgarity to "f**king."*

neanche per sogno
no way, lit. not even in a dream
Neanche per sogno ti presento mia cugina!
No way I'll introduce you to my cousin!

non esserci anima viva
to not be a living soul
Di domenica, non c'è anima viva nella città.
On Sundays, there isn't a living soul in the city.

quattro gatti
a few people, lit. four cats
Che brutta serata. C'erano soltanto quattro gatti nel nostro locale preferito.
What an awful evening. There were only a few people in our favorite night club.

pieno zeppo (di qualcosa)
crammed
Perché la pizzeria dietro l'angolo era piena zeppa, siamo andati in un fast-food.
Because the pizzeria around the corner was crammed, we went to a fast-food joint.

mare di qualcosa, m
sea of something
Da quando esce con Giulia, Leonardo affronta un mare di guai.
Since he's been going out with Giulia, Leonard has faced a sea of problems.

For sure the size of the sea gives an idea of a big quantity. Without being so big, un sacco, *"a bag"* or un mucchio, *"a pile,"* both give the same impression. When asked if you like something, you can answer: Mi piace un casino! *"I like it a brothel,"* or Mi piace un pacco, *"I like it a pack,"* or simply, A bomba! *"A bomb."*

15

cazzo (di niente), m
thing, lit. dick (of nothing)
Al lavoro Matthew non ha più un cazzo da fare.
At work Matthew has nothing to do anymore.

There are many ways to say "nothing." The easiest is to use synonyms of cazzo like un cavolo and un cavolo di niente, less offensive ways to describe "nothing." Other synonyms are un accidente and un bel niente, "an accident" and "a nice nothing." Some people will use a strange expression containing "a dried fig," un ficco secco, maybe because it lost all its volume when being dried. Non capire un "H," (acca) and non capire una mazza both mean to not understand a damn thing, lit. nothing, turned into an "H" and a (golf) club.

schifo, m
mess
Paolo dovresti prenderti una donna delle pulizie; il tuo appartamento è uno schifo.
Paolo, you should hire a cleaning lady; your flat is a mess.

porcheria, f/porcile, m
pigpen, pigsty
I tuoi amici vivono in una vera porcheria.
Your friends live in a real pigsty.

letamaio, m
pigsty, lit. pile of manure
Che letamaio il tuo appartamento!
What a pigsty your flat is!

Positive Feeling, the Youth Input

cannonata/figata, f
blast, lit. cannon shot/from figa, pussy
Il concerto di Massimo è stato una cannonata!
Massimo's concert was a blast!

cosmico, cosmica
amazing, lit. cosmic
È stata un'esperienza cosmica.
It was an amazing experience.

demenziale
crazy, a blast, lit. demented
La festa data da Paola era demenziale.
Paola's party was crazy.

essere la fine del mondo
to be the ___ to end all ___, lit. to be the end of the world
Milena mi ha fatto un pompino che era la fine del mondo.
Milena gave me the blow job to end all blow jobs.

galattico, galattica/megagalattico, megagalattica
cool/phat, lit. galactic
Gli amici di Nicoletta sono troppo galattici.
Nicoletta's friends are too cool.

mostruoso, mostruosa
sweet, cool, lit. monstrous
L'auto di Patrizio è mostruosa.
Patrizio's car is sweet.

pazzesco, pazzesca
incredible, awesome, lit. crazy

17

Venezia è una città pazzesca.
Venice is an incredible city.

pauroso, paurosa
frightening
Ha ereditato un pauroso mucchio di soldi da sua zia.
He inherited a frightening amount of money from his aunt.

da urlo
sexily, sexy, lit. from scream
Letizia indossava un vestito da urlo per il matrimonio di sua sorella.
Letizia had on a sexy dress at her sister's wedding.

di brutto
badly
Tamara si è fatta male di brutto in moto.
Tamara hurt herself badly on her motorcycle.

come un maiale
extremely, lit. as a pig
Cesare era felice come un maiale dopo l'esame di chimica.
Cesare was extremely happy after the chemistry exam.

The pig is the superlative animal per eccellenza. *The expression* come un maiale *changes the meaning of the adjective that precedes it. You can literally be fat as a pig, sad as a pig, happy as a pig, and of course dirty as a pig.*

a manetta
at max speed or volume, lit. to the lever

18

Quando Alfio mette la radio a manetta, i vicini si lamentano.
When Alfio plays the radio at max volume, the neighbors complain.

Other Important Stuff

esserci
to be almost done, lit. to be there
Ci siamo quasi. Mancano due minuti alla fine della lezione.
We're almost done. The lesson is over in two minutes.

fare
to go (to say), lit. to do
E a quel punto Susanna mi fa: "Vieni a casa mia!"
And at that point Susanna goes: "Come to my house!"

fare uno squillo a qualcuno
to call someone and ring once before hanging up, lit. to ring someone
Appena sei sotto casa mia fammi uno squillo!
Call me and ring once before hanging up as soon as you're in front of my house!

stare per
to be about to, lit. to stay for
Stavo per uscire di casa quando hai chiamato.
I was about to leave the house when you called.

bella lì
all right, lit. nice here
Bella lì, Paul. Ci vediamo domani in stazione.
All right, Paul. We'll meet tomorrow at the train station.

cazzata/cavolata, f

1. crap/nonsense; from *cazzo, cavolo*, dick
Non pensare più a questa cavolata.
Don't think about that crap anymore.

    or

2. serious/terrible thing
Harry ha fatto una cazzata a lasciare la moglie e i figli per una prostituta.
Harry did a terrible thing by leaving his wife and children for a prostitute.

stare bene a qualcuno

to serve someone right, lit. to be fine to someone
Non mi hai ascoltato e ti sei ammalato. Ti sta bene!
You didn't listen to me and you got sick. It serves you right!

CHAPTER THREE

La testa a posto:

Smart, Stupid, or Just Plain Nuts

Italy has taken much from American culture. It started with music and movies but has now progressed to adopting our politically correct ways. Nowadays in Italy, insulting people for their skin color, sexual orientation, or gender is tolerated less and less. The tendency to sue for libel and slander means that politically correct humor and insults now rule.

How can Italians then express their profound desire to put someone back in his place? As Italy provides the same level of education throughout the country, insulting someone's knowledge, skills or education is less dangerous. Italy has given the world great writers, scientists, artists, and architects. As a result, most Italians consider themselves more like Dante, Michelangelo, or Leonardo da Vinci than they probably deserve to.

When we pay attention to the world related to stupidity, Italian and French, two very close Latin languages, strongly differ. Italian prefers the family of *cazzo*, "dick," to express the lack of intelligence, while the romantic French links stupidity with *le con*, "pussy." In that regard Italian shows more respect to women (except in the south of the country where *la fessura*, "pussy," is the root of many words for stupidity). Maybe people should reconsider the cliché of Italians being macho and Frenchmen ladies' men.

Craziness and Mental Disorder

non avere tutte le rotelle a posto/avere qualche rotella fuori posto
to have a few screws loose, lit. to not have all cogs at their place/ to have some cogs out of place

Quando Malena parla, tutti si chiedono se ha qualche rotella fuori posto.

When Malena speaks, everyone wonders if she has a few screws loose.

dare i numeri
to talk nonsense, lit. to give the numbers

Katia non fa più caso a ciò che dice suo padre; da qualche giorno ormai dà i numeri.

Katia doesn't pay attention to what her father says anymore; he's been talking nonsense for a few days now.

pazzo, pazza da legare
berserk, lit. crazy to bind

Maurizio è diventato pazzo da legare quando ha visto sua moglie a letto con il suo migliore amico.

Maurizio went berserk when he saw his wife in bed with his best friend.

deragliare

to go crazy, lit. to derail

Non fare caso a ciò che dice mia zia. Quando è morto suo marito, ha deragliato.

Don't pay attention to what my aunt says. When her husband died, she went crazy.

essere fuori (di testa/melone)

to be crazy/out of one's mind, lit. to be out (of the head/melon)

Toni, sei troppo fuori.

Toni, you're completely out of your mind.

malato, malata

crazy, lit. ill

Salvatore, sei malato o soltanto scemo?

Salvatore, are you crazy or just dumb?

sciroccato, sciroccata

crazy; from *scirocco*, the southern wind from the Sahara that stifles Italy

Viviana, da quando sei caduta in moto sei un po' sciroccata.

Viviana, since you fell from your motorcycle, you've been a little crazy.

sclerare

to get crazy; from *sclerosi*, scleroses

Le costante lamentele della tua amica mi fanno sclerare.

Your friend's constant complaints are making me crazy.

svitato, svitata

screwy, lit. unscrewed

Bruno è un po' svitato ma mi piace molto.

Bruno is a bit screwy but I really like him a lot.

Intelligence and Stupidity

conoscere qualcosa come le proprie tasche
to know something like the back of one's hand, lit. to know something as well as one's pockets
Fidatevi dalla vostra guida; conosce questi sentieri come le proprie tasche.
Trust your guide; he knows these trails like the back of his hand.

cacasenno, m, f
know-it-all, smartass, lit. one who shits wisdom/good sense
Eh cacasenno, fammi un piacere e tieniti i tuoi pareri.
Hey smartass, do me a favor and keep your own opinions to yourself.

cacasentenze, m, f
moralist, one who acts like he/she is very smart, lit. one who shits sentences
I giovani non sopportano quando gli anziani fanno i cacasentenze.
Young people can't stand when the elderly play the moralist.

cima, f
expert, lit. peak
Maria ti può aiutare meglio di me; è una cima in quel campo.
Maria can help you better than me; she's an expert in that field.

Einstein, m
genius, Einstein
A scuola tutti i compagni di Paulo lo considerano un piccolo Einstein.
At school, all Paulo's classmates consider him a little genius.

sapientone, sapientona

whiz, lit. the big wise, scientist one

Tutti i maestri credono che Isabella sia una sapientona, invece bara a tutti gli esami.

Every single teacher believes Isabella is a whiz, but actually she cheats on every exam.

saccente, m

know-it-all; from *sapere*, to know

Dalle nostre parti, non ci piacciono i saccenti.

In our region, we don't like know-it-alls.

testa d'uovo, f

intellectual, nerd, lit. egghead

Arriva quella testa d'uovo di tua cugina . . . Scappiamo!

Your cousin, that nerd, is coming . . . Let's leave!

cervello/cervellone, m

mastermind, lit. big brain

Il cervellone della banda non è ancora stato beccato dalla polizia.

The gang's mastermind hasn't been caught by the police yet.

avere il cervello di segatura

to have sawdust for brains, lit. to have a sawdust brain

Federica sarà anche la ragazza più bella della valle ma ha il cervello di segatura.

Federica may be the cutest chick in the valley but she's got sawdust for brains.

non avere niente nella zucca

to have nothing upstairs, lit. to have nothing in the pumpkin

Aurelio reagisce in quel modo perchè non ha niente nella zucca.

Aurelio reacts that way because has nothing upstairs.

coglione, m

stupid, idiot, lit. testicle
Il nuovo sindaco è un noto coglione.
The new mayor is a famous idiot.

The dick is not the smartest organ, and a person that thinks with his dick is usually reduced to it. Il cazzo *and a lot of its regional variations, such as* la minchia, la pirla, il picio, *are in fact synonymous with idiot.* Una minchiata *is a dumb action and dummies are referred to using* che pirla! *or* che picio!

rincoglionire

to get senile, from *Coglione*, testicle
Quando diventano nonni, la maggiore parte dei genitori rincoglioniscono.
As soon as they become grandparents, most people get senile.

non capire un'acca/un tubo

to not understand a thing, lit. to not understand an "H"/a tube
Con tutto il dovuto rispetto, Professore, non capiamo un tubo alle Sue lezioni.
With all due respect, Professor, we don't understand a thing about your lessons.

goffo, goffa

clumsy, goofy
Tobias sarà anche molto intelligente ma quando deve fare qualcosa con le mani è molto goffo.
Tobias may be really clever, but when he has to use his hands he's very clumsy.

asino, asina/somaro, somara

cretin, lit. donkey

Siete tutti quanti somari, se non lottate per i vostri diritti.

You're all cretins if you don't fight for your rights.

According to the Bible, humans are the cleverest creation on Earth, and must rule over all the other animals. If animals accepted this without demonstrating any opposition, maybe they deserve the comparison humans make between some animals and the concept of idiocy. Donkeys are traditionally associated with stupidity. Stupid women will be called delle oche. L'oca, *"the goose," is seen as a dumb animal who makes a lot of noise for nothing. A slow person is* una persona veloce come un gatto di marmo, *literally "as fast as a marble cat," which expresses how slowly the information is processed. Humans recognize some positive qualities in animals (beside their flavor and the consistency of their flesh), as the following expression proves:* essere furbo come una volpe, *"to be as sly as a fox."*

---

babbeo, babbio, babbione, m

simple-minded, sucker, possibly from *barbaro*, barbaric

Un tipo ha proposto a Luigi il biglietto vincente della prossima lotteria e quel babbeo l'ha comprato.

A guy offered Luigi the winning ticket of the next lottery and that sucker bought it.

cretino, cretina

cretin

Cristina sei troppo cretina!
Cristina you're such a cretin!

deficiente, m, f/mongolo, mongola

idiot, lit. tarred/Mongol

Quel deficiente di mio cugino non mi ha ridato le chiavi di casa.
My cousin, that dummy, didn't give me back the house keys.

imbranato, imbranata

clumsy fool

Hai fatto cadere la mia nuova tazza del caffè, imbranata!
You dropped my new coffee cup, you clumsy fool!

salame, m

silly, naive person, lit. dried sausage

Sergio sei un salame se credi ancora che Tiziana ti sia fedele.
Sergio you're a fool if you still believe that Tiziana is faithful to you.

sciocco, sciocca

dummy

Quella sciocca di Debora ha dimenticato la valigia a casa.
Debora, that dummy, forgot her suitcase at home.

scemo, scema

idiot

Che scema; mia sorellina crede ancora a Babbo Natale.
What an idiot; my little sister still believes in Santa Claus.

CHAPTER FOUR

Ma ce l'hai il cazzo?:
Words to Both Flatter and Insult

Le parolacce, "bad words," and *le bestemmie*, "insults," are part of everyday Italian life. Speaking *bestemmie* used to be an unforgiveable crime; it was once said that if one man killed someone and another cursed God, only one of them would wind up in heaven...and you guessed it: that would be the murderer!

Street Italian is brimming with insults. You just have to sit on a schoolbus to *farsi l'orrecchio*. Or watch any Italian film. Wait with natives for a late *treno*, plane, or *autobus*. Anytime something goes wrong, and you'll see there are plenty of things that go wrong in Italy, instead of destroying someone's belongings or fighting, people express their rage verbally. Despite the screaming matches you may hear, violence is rare except after soccer games, political discussions, or more recently, at closed trash dumps near *Napoli*.

Aside from these issues, Italy did not get its reputation as *il paese della dolce vita* for nothing. By throwing insults around left and right, Italians can manage their fiery tempers with words alone. Escaping a bar fight with a wounded ego rather than a broken nose remains one of the country's big draws . . .

29

Insulting People

mostrare il dito medio a qualcuno
to give someone the middle finger, lit. to show the middle finger
to someone
La segretaria ha mostrato il dito medio al suo superiore e
ha lasciato l'ufficio.
The secretary gave her boss the finger and left the office.

farsi i cazzi propri
to mind one's own business, lit. to make one's own dicks
Ma perché non ti fai i cazzi tuoi?
Why don't you mind your own business?

mascalzone, m
rogue, rascal
Se Vittorio becca il mascalzone che gioca con il suo cam-
panello gli dà un paio di sberle.
*If Vittorio catches the rascal who is playing with his doorbell, he'll
slap him.*

pecora nera/mela marcia, f
black sheep, lit. rotten apple
In tutte le famiglie c'è una mela marcia.
In every family there's a black sheep.

sacco di merda, m
scumbag, lit. bag of shit
Eh sacco di merda, muoviti.
Hey, scumbag, move it.
Lit. Hey scumbag, move yourself.

pidocchio, m
cockroach, scumbag, lit. lice

30

Levati dalle palle, pidocchio!
Get lost, cockroach!
Lit. Get off my balls, lice!

bastardo, bastarda
bastard
Bastardi, ridatemi i miei vestiti!
Bastards, give me my clothes back!

Bastardo *is a word you will ordinarily hear in a group of friends. Young people may call each other* bastardi *for different reasons. If someone pulls a prank, he's a* bastardo *too. To show he already knows it, a typical* italiano *will claim he's* un bastardo dentro, *"a bastard inside," while beating his heart twice with the right hand. Originally* bastardo *meant "illegitimate," and in a very Catholic country, where* la famiglia *was the center of society, it was one of the worst things you could call someone. Rest assured, you'll always find someone ready to remind you of this historical fact! Call someone this name and take a free tour of the Italian ER.*

cornuto, cornuta
cuckhold
Cornuto! Tua moglie si fa tutti.
Loser! Your wife does everyone.
Cuckhold! Your wife does everyone.

Cornuto, cornuta, *and* fare le corna *all come from* corna, *"horn." In addition to being used to insult hot-blooded males, words for cuckhold also denote a very lucky* person, the kind who wins every card game. Such an amount of luck must be, in the popular vision, counterbalanced by some infidelity from his/her partner. Cornuto *may also mean "dummy," "idiot," and so on. But in Italy, where women are supposed to stick to tradition and follow certain rules, one may take it a tad too seriously. In 2007, one man sued another who called him a* cornuto *in public. The victim won the case—as well as 500 euro! We don't know if it saved the wife's reputation or the husband's, but be warned to use this word carefully or carry a lot of cash with you.*

faccia di culo/merda, f
asshole, lit. face of ass/shit
Faccia di merda, vaffanculo!
Go f**k yourself, asshole!

testa di cazzo, f
dickhead
Se ti prendo t'ammazzo, testa di cazzo!
If I catch you I'll kill you, dickhead!

stronzo, stronza
bastard, son of a bitch, lit. turd-head
Due stronzi hanno picchiato Sacha alla fermata del bus, senza nessun motivo.
Two bastards beat Sacha at the bus stop for no reason.

figlio, figlia di puttana/buona donna
son of a bitch, lit. son/daughter of a whore/good lady
Siamo tutti figli di puttane.
We're all a bunch of s.o.b.s.

figlio, figlia di mignotta
bastard, lit. son/daughter of an unknown mother
Che figlio di mignotta mi ha rubato le chiavi del motorino!
That bastard stole the keys to my scooter!

vacca, f
slut, bitch, whore, lit. cow
La tua ragazza si comporta da vacca.
Your girlfriend is acting like a slut.

prendiculo, m, f
full of shit, lit. ass-taker
Non fidarti di Adam, è un prendiculo.
Don't trust Adam, he's full of shit.

vaffanculo/vaff'
go f**k yourself, lit. go get f**ked/go take a bath
Vaffanculo a te, a tuo padre e a tua sorella!
Go f**k yourself!
Lit. Go get f**ked, your father and your sister too!

vaffanbagno
go to Hell, lit. go take a bath
Vaffanbagno a te, nonna!
Go to Hell, grandma!

andare a cagare
to go f**k oneself, lit. to go take a shit
Andate tutti a cagare! Non vi voglio più vedere.
All of you go f**k yourselves! I don't want to see you anymore.

andare a letto
to get lost, lit. to go to bed
Vai a letto, va'. Stai dicendo troppe fesserie.
Get lost. You're talking too much bullshit.

Bestemmie and Interjections

porca puttana vacca troia
f**king A, f**k, lit. filthy whore cow sow
Porca puttana vacca troia! Mi sono ancora scordato l'anniversario di matrimonio!
F**king A! Once again I forgot the anniversary!

cazzo, cazzerola
f**k
Cazzo, Dolores! Dove sei andata? Ti ho aspettato per mezz'ora!
F**k, Dolores! Where have you been? I've been waiting for half an hour.

emme
shoot, lit. "m," first letter of *merda*
Emme! Tutti i negozi sono chiusi, e non c'e niente da bere per la festa!
Shoot! All the shops are closed, and there's nothing to drink for the party.

mannaggia
damn, darn
Mannaggia, è già ora di tornare al lavoro. Come vola il tempo!
Darn, it's already time to go back to work. How time flies!

merda
shit
Merda, Marinella! Taci quando parlo.
Shit, Marinella! Shut up when I'm talking.

porca miseria
bloody hell, lit. (filthy) pig misery
Porca miseria rispondimi! Cosa c'è che non va?
Bloody hell, answer me! What's wrong?

porca puttana
f**king hell, lit. (filthy) pig whore
Porca puttana, Tito doveva essere qui due ore fa, ancora non si è fatto vivo.
F**king hell, Tito had to be here two hours ago, and hasn't shown up yet.

porca troia
f**king hell, lit. (filthy) pig sow
Porca troia, a Susanna è mancato un numero alla lotteria per essere milionaria.
F**king hell, Susanna was missing only one number at the lottery to become a millionaire.

porca vacca
shit, lit. (filthy) pig cow
Non trovo più le chiavi della macchina. Porca vacca, Samanta, dove le hai messe?
I can't find my car keys. Shit, Samanta, where did you put them?

porco cane
damn it, lit. (filthy) pig dog
Porco cane, se il tassista non accelera, perderemo il treno.
Damn it, if the taxi driver doesn't go faster, we'll miss the train.

porca l'oca/oca
damn it, lit. (filthy) pig goose
Porca l'oca, siamo ancora in ritardo per la lezione!
Damn, we're going to be late for the lesson!

porco Dio

Goddamn it, lit. (filthy) pig god

Porco Dio, la vuoi piantare?

Goddamn it, knock that off!

lit. Pig god, do you want to plant it now?

porca madonna

Jesus, Christ

Porca Madonna, siamo salvi per un pelo!

Jesus, we're saved by the bell!

Cristo

Christ

Basta! Cristo, non ti fermi mai di parlare?

Enough! Jesus, don't you ever stop talking?

diobestia/Dio cane

damn, lit. God beast/God dog

Diobestia! Ho dimenticato una valigia nel baule del taxi!

Damn! I forgot one suitcase in the trunk of the taxi!

mortacci tuoi/li mortacci

go to hell!, lit. (may) your dead people (be damned)

Mortacci tuoi, Ugo! Ciò che hai fatto è imperdonabile.

Go to Hell, Ugo! What you did is unforgivable.

CHAPTER FIVE

A manetta:

On the Road Again

Italian design and knowledge created artworks like Piaggio's funny three-wheeled *Ape* (bee) or its mythic *Vespa* (wasp), now true Italian emblems. Italians though, also have strong relationships with their cars. They may live in ugly blocks of flats in the *inquinati* suburbs, but *l'auto* always has to look perfect. Men, in particular, may spend hours cleaning their cars. And it doesn't surprise the authors when considering the macho use they make out of it. A car is like a business card, and often used to *rimorchiare le ragazze*, "seduce chicks." With low salaries, Italians tend to live with their parents until marriage. As they can't afford hotel rooms for their significant or not so significant others, cars are used for another purpose.

But when it comes to actually driving, Italian cities abide by the "Law of the Jungle." Try to take a taxi ride in Naples, or to cross any city by car; you will have to forget all the traffic laws you've learned and be a more than an attentive driver. You'll be passed from either the left or right side. You will wonder if traffic lights are just *decorazioni natalizie*, if horns shouldn't be banned, and if that f**king jerk couldn't stop his car somewhere other than in the middle of *la strada* to get his cigarettes. One fact is certain: every time you can be *sorpassato*, "passed," you will be! It's sad to say, but if you really care about *pedoni*, "pedestrians," you shouldn't stop to let them cross the road; the car behind you will take the opportunity to pass you and make a strike instead. All the above can likely be explained by the *Ferrari*, *Cagiva*, and *Ducati* phenomenons—Italians are very proud of their national cars and motorcycles and sometimes forget the difference between driving and racing.

chiedere un passaggio
to ask for a lift
Ho chiesto a Domenico un passaggio fino alla stazione.
I asked Domenico for a lift to the railway station.

fare l'autostop
to hitchhike
Se sei una ragazza è più facile fare l'autostop.
If you're a girl it's easier to hitchhike.

dare uno strappo/un passaggio
to give a ride, lit. to give a rip/a passage
Salta su, ti do un passaggio fino al prossimo paese.
Come in, I'll give you a ride to the next village.

razzo, m
race car, lit. rocket
Occhio, arriva Stefano col suo razzo.
Careful, Stefano is arriving with his race car.

aver un volante di ghisa
to drive very slowly, lit. to have a cast-iron steering wheel
Davide ha un volante di ghisa.
Davide drives very slowly.

freccia, f

turn signal lit. arrow

Metti la freccia quando giri!

Use the turn signal when you turn!

truccato, truccata

souped-up; from *trucco*, make-up, trick

Marisa andare in giro con un vecchio motorino truccato.

Marisa rides around on an old, souped-up scooter.

fare due passi

to go for a walk, lit. to make two steps

Facciamo due passi fuori, ti devo dire qualcosa.

Let's go for a walk outside, I have to tell you something.

rottame, m

lemon, lit. wreck

Non vorrai mica comprare questo rottame?

Don't tell me you want to buy this lemon?

carretta, f

jalopy, lit. little cart

Se Mario va da solo a comprare la macchina, tornerà con una carretta.

If Mario goes alone to buy a car, he'll come back with a jalopy.

The time spent cleaning one's car in Italy is impressive. While not everyone can afford a new car, every person can manage to have a clean one. Still, old cars are made fun of regularly and even the noises they make have inspired some fun slang. It may be difficult to listen to the radio if you take a ride in un macinino, *"a little miller," or in* un vio-lino, *"a violin."* Bagnarola *is a word from the central Italy*

dialects that may come from the French slang for car, bagnole. *The general appearance of a used car may recall* una carcassa, *"a carcass,"* or un bidone *or* una pattumiera, *"a can" or "a trash can." Lemons are also called* un ferrovecchio, *lit. "an old iron." One thing is for sure though, you'll learn that even with a lemon, Italian men can drive quickly and dangerously,* in modo spericolato. *Enjoy the ride.*

fare una capatina/scappata

to stop by, lit. to make a little escapade

Se passate per Firenze, fate una scappata a casa mia.

If you pass through Florence, stop by my house.

andare a zonzo/andare qua e là

to wander around, lit. to go here and there

Invece di andare a zonzo, perché non leggi un libro?

Instead of wandering around, why don't you read a book?

sfrecciare come un fulmine

to dart, lit. to dart as a lightning

L'auto della polizia sfrecciava come un fulmine ma non è stata sufficientemente veloce per prendere i ladri.

The police car darted, but it wasn't fast enough to catch the thieves.

pantera, f

fast police car, lit. panther

Dopo aver dato la caccia ai criminali, la pantera della polizia era buona da rottamare.

After it chased the criminals, the fast police car was good to throw away.

sgommare

to burn rubber, drive very fast; from *gomma*, gum

Ad Alessandro piace sgommare in tutte le curve.
Alessandro loves to burn rubber on all the curves.

testacoda, m
180°, lit. head-tail
L'auto ha fatto un testacoda sull'autostrada. Per fortuna non c'era traffico.
The car did a 180° on the highway. Thank God, there was no traffic.

tagliare la strada a qualcosa
to cut in front of someone, lit. to cut the road
Dopo il sorpasso vietato, l'autista spericolato ci ha tagliato la strada.
After the illegal passing, the reckless driver cut in front of us.

fare benzina
to fill up, lit. to make gasoline
Se non troviamo subito un posto per fare benzina, ci toccherà spingere la macchina.
If we don't find a place to fill up the car, we'll have to push it.

andare ad occhio/a naso/a caso
to go/follow one's instincts, lit. to go at eye/nose/random
Nessuno di noi conosceva la strada per venire a casa tua, ma siamo andati a caso e ci è andato di culo.
None of us knew the way to come to your house, but we followed our instincts and we got lucky.

Time and Distance

guidare come una lumaca/tartaruga
to drive like a snail, lit. to drive like a snail/turtle

L'avvocato guida come una tartaruga.
The lawyer drives like a snail.

a tutta birra
very fast, lit. to all beer
Fabio guida sempre a tutta birra.
Fabio always drives very fast.

andare a manetta/smanettare
to throttle; from *manetta*, throttle
**Nicolao andava a manetta anche nelle curve cieche . . .
Spericolato!**
Nicolao throttled it on blind curves too . . . Reckless!

a un tiro di schioppo
a stone's throw, lit. within a gunshot
**La sua casa di vacanza si trova ad un tiro di schioppo del
mare.**
His holiday home is a stone's throw from the sea.

fare il giro dell'oca
to go on a long detour, lit. to make the tour of the goose
Hanno fatto il giro dell'oca per trovare un parcheggio.
They went on a long detour to find a parking spot.

metterci una vita
to take forever to do something, lit. to put one's life on something
**Cesare, Anna, ci avete messo una vita ad arrivare! La festa
è quasi finita.**
*Cesare, Anna, it took you forever to get here! The party is almost
over.*

in un battibaleno
in a flash

Ho sentito le grida e sono uscito di casa in un battibaleno.
I heard the shouts and left the house in a flash.

da un pezzo (di tempo)

for ages, lit. from a piece (of time)
Naomi e Sandra non si sono più viste da un pezzo.
Naomi and Sandra haven't seen each other for ages.

come ai vecchi tempi

like in the old days
Tutto ritornerà come ai vecchi tempi.
Everything will come back like in the old days.

allungare il passo

to hurry up, lit. to stretch out the step
Ragazzi, sarebbe meglio allungare il passo adesso, prima
che cali la notte.
Dudes, it'd be better to hurry up now, before it's dark.

per farla breve

in other words, lit. make it short
Per farla breve, abbiamo girato cento negozi ma abbiamo
trovato la gonna che volevo.
*In other words, we went to a hundred shops but finally found the
dress I wanted.*

a raffica

a mile a minute, lit. at blow
Guido sparava stronzate a raffica.
Guido spewed bullshit a mile a minute.

dalla a alla z

from a to z
Ti racconteremo tutto dalla a alla z.
We'll tell you everything from a to z.

43

di corsa

in a hurry, lit. in a run

Quando Diana ha saputo del matrimonio di Walter, è partita di corsa in camera sua.

When Diana heard about Walter's wedding, she went to her room in a hurry.

mettere radici/fare la muffa

to wait for hours, lit. to put roots/to make mold

Tutti stavano mettendo radici, quando finalmente la sposa arrivò e la cerimonia incominciò.

Everyone was waiting for hours, when finally the bride came and the ceremony began.

ora di punta, f

rush hour, lit. peak hour

Durante l'ora di punta, è meglio viaggiare con la metropolitana. Milano è troppo incasinata.

During rush hour, it's better to travel by subway. Milan is such a mess.

al volo

immediately, lit. to the flight

Se non capite al volo, siete cretini.

If you don't understand it immediately, you're dummies.

in un batter d'occhio

in the blink of an eye

In un batter d'occhio, il rapitore aveva afferrato un bambino che giocava nel parco.

In the blink of an eye, the kidnapper grabbed a child who was playing in the park.

in quattro e quattro otto

as fast as lightning, lit. in four plus four eights

In quattro e quattro otto ha preso la sua roba ed é sparito.

He took his stuff as fast as lightning and disappeared.

saltare qualcosa (turno, pagamento, pranzo . . .)

to skip something

Marinella, se non fai i compiti, salti la cena.

Marinella, if you don't do your homework, you'll skip dinner.

in mezzo al nulla

in the middle of nowhere

Siamo stati fortunati a trovare un albergo qui in mezzo al nulla.

We were lucky to have found a hotel here in the middle of nowhere.

a casa di Dio/a ca' di Dio

far away, remote place, lit. at God's house

Quanto vorrei che i vicini abitassero a casa di Dio.

How delightful it would be if the neighbors lived far away.

in culo ai lupi

in bum-f**k Egypt, lit. in ass of the wolves

Sarà anche una casa con tanto charme, ma in culo ai lupi, io non ci vado a vivere!

It may be a house with a lot of charm, but I don't want to live in bum-f**k Egypt!

anno luce, m

years, lit. light year

Cosa ci raccontate di bello ragazze? Sono anni luce che non ci vediamo!

What's new, girls? We haven't seen each other for years!

CHAPTER SIX

Cosa bolle in pentola:

Food, Glorious Food

No need to be an expert in art, architecture, or history to appreciate Italy's finest creations. Some might say a delicious *tiramisù* beats *il Davide*, Michelangelo's David, any day. Although Italy has many famous dishes, its crowning achievement is undoubtedly *pasta*. According to recent statistics, Italy produces more than 75 percent of the pasta you'll eat in Europe and is the biggest producer worldwide. Italians each eat something like 28 kg of pasta a year, the world champions, while Americans eat only 9 kg. Imagination gave hundreds of shapes, sizes, consistencies, and recipes to this wheat specialty. Serious studies are made to find the perfect pasta that sticks best to sauce, takes the least time to cook, and stays *al dente*. *La pasta fatta in casa*, "homemade pasta," is surely the best you'll ever eat.

Le mamme italiane, "Italian mothers," are experts in the *tradizione* of their country's cuisine. Many say that women have two ways of keeping their husbands at home: sex or food. Past a certain age, some skills are better kept than others! Hence traditional *Italiane* spend a lot of time in the kitchen. *Le mamme* put a spell on their men, and the magic words are *lasagna, spaghetti, penne, pasta al forno*, and the sauces that go with them: *salsa al ragù*, also known as *bolognese* (outside *Bologna*), *al pesto*, *alla putanesca*, *aglio-olio-peperoncino*, *alle vongole*, *alla carbonara*, *all'arrabbiata* . . . Perhaps this is the reason Italy had one of Europe's lowest divorce rates for most of the past hundred years (it could've also been the fact that divorce was illegal). In any case, stuffed with pasta, many husbands never leave; at least not before they have digested . . . which can take awhile.

Cooking and Eating

fare venire l'acquolina in bocca (a qualcuno)
to make someone's mouth water, lit. to make the little water come to mouth
I sapori che escono dalla tua cucina mi fanno venire l'acquolina in bocca.
The smells coming from your kitchen make my mouth water.

peccato di gola, m
sweets, lit. throat sin
Marilyn non sa resistere ai peccati di gola.
Marilyn can't resist sweets.

ghiotto, ghiotta
to love (food); from *gola*, throat
Mike è ghiotto di cannoli.
Mike loves cannoli.

fare la pappa
to cook, lit. to make the baby food
Adesso la nonna ti fa la pappa.
Now your grandmother will cook for you.

paninoteca, f

snack bar, lit. collection of sandwiches

Ci diamo sempre appuntamento alla paninoteca della stazione.

We always meet up at the snack bar at the railway station.

chimico, m

fast food restaurant, lit. chemical

Ragazzi, andiamo a mangiare dal chimico stasera?

Dudes, are we eating fast food tonight?

Fast food restaurants have done their best to infiltrate Europe. So no worries . . . what a relief it will be to eat a processed, precooked hamburger when you tire of the homemade risotto, lasagna, and pizza those crazy Italians prefer to Mickey D's. Not all Italians welcomed this fast food invasion with open arms. The leader of the resistance was a certain Carlo Petrini. In 1986 he started the Slow Food movement. Slow Food aims to educate the public about the culinary sciences, save traditional products, maintain biodiversity, and promote a new relation to food which creates a real bond between customers and producers. The movement is present on five continents but remains quite small, with only 80,000 members, more than half of whom are Italian. It seems a remake of David vs. Goliath: may history repeat itself!

boccone/bocconcino, m

bite, lit. mouthful/little mouthful

Gli daresti un bocconcino della tua pizza?

Would you give him a bite of your pizza?

beccolare
to eat slowly; from *becco*, beak
Se continui a beccolare, diventa tutto freddo.
If you continue to eat so slowly, it'll get cold.

foraggiare
to give food, lit. to give fodder
In questo istituto foraggiano gli studenti con cibi macrobiotici.
In this institute they feed the students macrobiotic meals.

foraggio, m
food, lit. fodder
Il foraggio che ci davano da mangiare faceva schifo.
The food they fed us was disgusting.

magnare (Centro, Sud)
to eat, in *Romano*
Non c'è niente da magnare.
There's nothing to eat.

mangiare a sbafo
to eat for free
Se pensate di mangiare a sbafo nel mio locale, sognate.
If you think you can eat for free in my restaurant, you're dreaming.

sbafare (Centro)
to gobble
Carlo si é sbafato tutta la torta!
Carlo ate all the pie by himself.

pappare/papparsi
to eat; from *pappa*
Non vi abbiamo lasciato niente; abbiamo pappato tutto.
We didn't leave you anything; we ate everything.

qualcosa da mettere sotto i denti

something to eat, lit. something to put under the teeth

Stefania cerca qualcosa da mettersi sotto i denti ma il suo ragazzo si è scordato di fare la spesa.

Stefania is looking for something to eat, but her boyfriend forgot to go grocery shopping.

spazzare/spazzolare

to devour, lit. to brush

Marco ha spazzato tutta la pasta in pochi minuti.

Marco devoured all the pasta in a just a few minutes.

allupato, allupata

hungry (also for sex), lit. turned into a wolf

È talmente allupato che si mangerebbe una mucca intera.

He's so hungry that he could eat a whole cow.

mangiarsi anche le gambe del tavolo

to be starving, lit. to eat even the legs of the table

I bambini di Claudia avrebbero mangiato anche le gambe del tavolo.

Claudia's children were starving.

empirsi/riempirsi le budella

to fill one's belly, to stuff oneself, lit. to fill one's guts

Dopo essersi empiti le budella per circa tre ore, i turisti tedeschi hanno finalmente deciso di partire.

After the German tourists had filled their bellies for almost three hours, they finally decided to leave.

pieno, piena come un uovo

stuffed, lit. as full as an egg

Dopo questa mangiata, Mirco era pieno come un uovo.

After that huge meal, Mirco was stuffed.

avere uno stomaco da struzzi

to have a strong stomach, lit. to have an ostrich stomach

Devi avere uno stomaco da struzzi per non essere ancora stato male dopo tutto quel che hai inghiottito.

You must have a strong stomach: you're not sick after all that you swallowed.

Just a Little More and Far Too Much

ghiotto, ghiotta

glutton, gluttonous; from *gola*, throat

Tina è ghiottissima di cioccolata al whisky.

Tina is a glutton for whiskey-flavored chocolate.

fogna, f

pig, glutton, lit. sewer

Sei proprio una fogna per mangiare tutte queste schifezze.

You're such a glutton to eat all that junk food.

mangiata pantagruelica, f

huge meal, from the main character of a Rabelais's play Pantagruel

Dopo la mangiata pantagruelica, gli invitati non potevano più alzarsi dalle loro sedie.

After the huge meal, the guests couldn't move their asses from their chairs.

abbuffata/abboffata, f (Sud)

huge meal

Il cenone di Capodanno sarà un'abbuffata, come al solito.

New Year's Eve dinner is going to be a huge meal, as usual.

abbuffarsi (Sud)

to eat a lot/like pigs

Alla festa di compleanno di Giulia ci siamo tutti abbuffati di brutto.

At Giulia's birthday party, we all ate like pigs.

mangiare come un maiale/porco

to eat like a pig

Elio mangia come un maiale.

Elio eats like a pig.

mangiarsi una mucca intera

to eat a horse, lit. to eat oneself a whole cow

Sono talmente affamato che potrei mangiarmi una mucca intera.

I'm so hungry I could eat a horse.

scorpacciata, f

huge meal

Non posso dire che a casa dei Rossi abbiamo fatto una scorpacciata: io ho ancora fame, e tu?

I can't say we had a huge meal at the Rossi's house: I'm still hungry, and you?

mangiare come un lupo/uccellino

to eat like a wolf/little bird

In casa degli altri, mio marito mangia come un uccellino, mentre da noi mangia come un lupo.

At other's houses my husband eats very little, while at home he eats like a wolf.

spuntino, m

snack

Arrivati in cima alla montagna, ci faremo uno spuntino.
Once we get to the top of the mountain, we'll have a snack.

mangiucchiare
to snack; from *mangiare*, to eat
Smetti di mangiucchiare o non avrai più fame per cena.
Stop snacking or you won't be hungry for dinner.

Italy is not the best place to start a diet. You'll be con-
stantly tempted by the delicious smells of panini, gelati
artigianali, pizze al trancio, and pasticcini. There's nothing
you can do—you'll snack and you'll enjoy it. However, in
order to take advantage of these culinary delights, you
must enlarge your vocabulary. You'll consider snacking
almost an exercise. Don't say sto facendo uno spuntino,
I'm having a snack, anymore. Switch to sto sbocconcel-
lando, sto (s)piluccando, or sto sgranocchiando instead.

---

fare la scarpetta
to suck up the sauce with a piece of bread, lit. to make the little shoe
Luigi, non far la scarpetta nei ristoranti gastronomici.
Luigi, don't soak up the sauce with a piece of bread in fancy
restaurants.

Leaving the Table

scoreggia, f
noisy fart
La scoreggia può mettere allegria.
A noisy fart can make people laugh.

loffa, f
smelly fart
Mamma che puzza! Chi ha mollato 'sta loffa?
What a stink! Who let out that smelly fart?

fare una puzza/puzzetta
to fart, lit. to make a stink
Il piccolo Alex sta facendo un sacco di puzzette.
Little Alex is farting a lot.

cesso, m
toilet, John, loo
Devo andare al cesso, fammi passare!
I have to go to the John, let me through!

cacatoio, m
public toilets, shithole; from *cacare*, to shit
Questa casa è talmente sporca; sembra un calcatoio.
This house is so dirty; it's a real shithole.

scappare qualcosa a qualcuno
to have to do something, lit. to escape something to someone
Mi scappa la pipì.
I have to pee.

sciolta, f
runs; from *sciogliere*, to melt
Ogni volta che mangio a casa tua, mi viene la sciolta . . .
Every time I eat at your house, I get the runs . . .

caghetta, f
shits, lit. little shit
Sono tornato dall'Africa con la caghetta.
I came back from Africa with the shits.

CHAPTER SEVEN

Superalcolizzato:

Beer Before Liquor . . .

The Roman Empire expanded its culture as well as its *viticoltura*, the science and study of vines (wine-producing grapevines), toward their newly conquered territories. Still today, Italy is known world-wide for its delicious wines. These wines can be found all over the country, from robust chianti to melt-in-your-mouth *brunello di Montalcino.* While many specifics go into making wine, the quality of soil, climate, and winemaking knowledge give Italian wines their *je ne sais quoi.* Winemaking in Italy is as popular as ever: each year celebrities or rich foreigners "follow their dreams" and buy vineyards in Italy. Often, the vineyards are redone and then replanted by wines the foreign owners prefer rather than indigenous *vitigni,* "varietals." This wreaks havoc on traditional wine production and defeats biodiversity. Even worse, these ex-pats will write a book about their experience of redoing an old *casa* and vineyard in Italy, and God forbid, it will be turned into a sappy movie.

With its regional production of wines and liquors, such as *grappa, amari,* and different digestive spirits, as well as its warm summer nights, Italy will tempt you to overindulge in its alcoholic specialties. Keep in mind the old saying: *leoni di sera, pecore di mattina*, "lions at night, sheep in the morning." Or the hipper version: *la sera leoni, la mattina coglioni,* lit. "at night lions, in the morning dummies."

Have a Drink

avere la gola secca
to be thirsty, lit. to have a dry throat
Ho la gola secca; dammi da bere.
I'm thirsty; give me something to drink.

crepare/morire di sete
to die of thirst
Tanti vecchietti sono crepati di sete durante le canicole.
Many old fogeys died of thirst during the last heat wave.

turno/giro di bevute, m
round, lit. turn of drinks
Evviva! Il prossimo turno è offerto dal padrone.
Wonderful! The next round is offered by the barkeeper.

birrino, m
beer, lit. little beer
Cameriera, arriva 'sto birrino? Ho la gola secca!
Waitress, where's my beer? I'm thirsty!

cicchetto/cicchettino, m
little glass
Dante ci ha offerto un cicchetto di limoncino.
Dante offered us a little glass of limoncino.

or

grappa, liqueur

Ci hanno offerto un cicchettino alla fine del pranzo.
They offered us a grappa at the end of the meal.

corretto, corretta

with a splash of liquor, lit. corrected

Come fa a bere caffé corretto a colazione?
How can he drink coffee with a splash of liquor at breakfast?

vinaccia, f

bad quality, cheap wine, vinegar. *Vinaccia* is the grape residue
left after pressing out the juice to make wine. It is distilled to
make grappa.

Vai al supermercato e comprami vino, non vinaccia.
Go to the supermarket and get me wine, not vinegar.

sapere di tappo

spoiled (due to a bad cork which lets the wine oxygenate), lit. that
tastes of cork

Prendi un'altra bottiglia in cantina. Questa sa di tappo.
Go get another bottle in the cellar. This one is spoiled.

vinello, m

light wine, lit. little wine

Non è niente male questo vinello!
This light wine is not so bad!

dare alla testa/picchiare

to give a headache, lit. to give to the head/to hit

Non comprare questo vino; picchia.
Don't buy this wine; it'll give you a headache.

superalcolico, m

hard alcohol, lit. super alcoholic beverage

Non si dovrebbe mai iniziare una festa con superalcolici.

One should never start a party with hard alcohol.

tazzare

to drink (alcohol), lit. to mug

Pino e Martino hanno tazzato per tutto il giorno.

Pino and Martino drank all day long.

buttare giù un paio di bicchieri

to have a drink or two, lit. to throw down a pair of glasses

Italo ha buttato giù un paio di bicchieri con Tiziana dopo il lavoro.

Italo had a drink or two with Tiziana after work.

bere d'un fiato

to chug, lit. to drink in one breath

Non bere questo bicchiere di vino tutto d'un fiato; apprezzalo.

Don't chug this glass of wine; appreciate it.

trincare (Nord)

to drink; from the German *trinken*, to drink

I tuoi amici si sono trincati mezza bottiglia della mia grappa.

Your friends drank half my bottle of grappa.

bere come una spugna

to drink like a fish, lit. to drink like a sponge

Samuele beve come una spugna.

Samuele drinks like a fish.

vecchia spugna, f

wino, lit. old sponge

Eh vecchia spugna, come te la passi?
Hey wino, how you doin'?

Getting and Being Drunk

prendersi una ciucca
to get smashed/wasted, lit. to take oneself to drunkenness
Stasera Emilio compie diciotto anni e si prenderà una ciucca.
Tonight Emilio turns eighteen and he's going to get completely wasted.

alcolizzarsi
to get dead drunk; from *alcolizzato*, wino
Tutti i fine settimana, gli studenti si alcolizzano di brutto.
Every weekend, students get dead drunk.

essere fuori come un balcone
to be drunk as a skunk, lit. to be out like a balcony
Ogni volta che vedo Vanessa è fuori come un balcone.
Each time I see Vanessa she's drunk as a skunk.

ubriaco fradicio/marcio
blind-drunk, lit. rotten drunk
Un barbone ubriaco fradicio disturba tutto il vicinato.
A blind-drunk wino is disturbing the entire neighborhood.

No matter which language you look at, alcohol and its devastating effects inspire a lot of slang and colloquial expressions. People get smashed literally in expressions like, disfato, *"destroyed,"* sberlato, *"slapped," and*

andare in botta *(in* pisano, *the dialect from Pisa), "to go in barrel." Often drunkenness is accompanied by strange behaviors that have also given rise to interesting idiomatic expressions. Winos, occasional drinkers, and binge drinkers can do crazy things. Those commenting on their situation will say* sono fuori *(come un balcone), "they're out (as a balcony)," or* sono andati/partiti, *"they're gone." Filth is also associated with this kind of behavior in expressions like,* sono concio, *"I'm dirty," and* sono concio da fare paura, *"I'm scary dirty." In every case, the drunk person is no longer the same and actually doesn't give a shit about others' opinions.*

---

sbronzo, sbronza
drunk, lit. drunkenness
Siete tornati sbronzi al lavoro dopo la pausa pranzo.
You came back to work drunk after the lunch break.

The Day after Yesterday

lingua felpata, f
cotton mouth, lit. smooth tongue
Il giorno dopo la festa, ci siamo svegliati con la lingua felpata.
The day after the party, we woke up with cotton mouth.

farsi passare la sbronza/sbornia/ciucca
to sober up, lit. to make oneself pass the drunkenness
Per farsi passare la sbornia, Antonio beve sempre un infuso di alloro.
To sober up, Antonio always drinks an infusion of bay leaves.

doposbronza, m

hangover, lit. after drunkenness

Bere è bello, ma il doposbronza fa male.

Drinking is nice, but the hangover hurts.

sboccare

to throw up, lit. to unmouth

Al bar, una ragazza totalmente fatta ha sboccato sui pantaloni di Pietro.

At the bar, a girl who was completely trashed threw up on Pietro's pants.

fare i gattini

to barf/blow chunks, lit. to make kittens

Se i tuoi amici continuano a bere stasera, finiranno per fare i gattini.

If your friends go on drinking tonight, they'll end up barfing.

dare di stomaco

to throw up, lit. to give from the stomach

Jennifer può di solito bere almeno cinque birre senza dare di stomaco.

Jennifer can normally drink at least five beers without throwing up.

CHAPTER EIGHT

Come stai?:
Expressing Your Ups and Downs

You may already have noticed that Italy is a macho country. As a result, expressing one's ups and downs is not well tolerated, especially if you're a man. That doesn't mean Italians don't have feelings. It is common knowledge that Italians speak *con le mani*, "with their hands." Sounds and signs precede the use of language and serve as giveaways to feelings and emotions. *Le interiezioni*, "interjections," can be basic, but they're still the secret knowledge of a community and aren't normally shared with foreigners. Italians express disgust with *puah* or *beh*, boredom with *uff* or *uffa*. *Mah* or *boh* communicate doubt while *toh* or *oh* announce surprise. Unpleasant surprises will be accompanied with *Accidenti!* (literally "Mishaps!") the equivalent of "Rats!" or "Shoot!" To cry out in pain, Italians will use *ahi*, *uhi*, *ahimè* rather than the English "Ow!"

Expressing feelings in this country can be considered taboo or a sign of weakness. When taboo is involved and when weakness is present, slang and colloquial expressions are just around the corner.

Fear factor

fifa, f

cowardice

La fifa non sempre si può superare.

Cowardice can't always be beaten.

tremarella, f

fear, shakes; from *tremare*, to shake

Quando l'arbitro vide i tifosi corrergli dietro, gli è venuta la tremarella.

When the referee saw the fans running after him, he got the shakes.

pelle d'oca, f

goosebumps, lit. goose skin

Raccontami una storia che dia la pelle d'oca!

Tell me a story that gives me goosebumps!

avere le gambe che fanno Giacomo Giacomo

to have legs that are shaking, lit. to have the legs that make Giacomo Giacomo

Quando ho detto a Lisa che ero follemente innamorato di lei avevo le gambe che facevano Giacomo Giacomo.

When I told Lisa I was crazy in love with her, my legs were shaking.

Fear is one of the first sensazioni; *it pushed human beings to develop ways to protect themselves from* nemici, *"enemies," and danger. Fear makes the body talk in a physiological language that in some circumstances, we'd*

prefer it keep silent. To be scared in slang is translated into pisciarsi addosso dalla paura, *"to piss on one-self from fear." There are also expressions similar to the English "to shit one's pants." Italians will* cagarsi addosso (dalla paura), *"to shit on oneself (from fear),"* cagarsi sotto, *"to shit under oneself," or* farsela sotto, *"to do it under oneself." No wonder dogs can tell when human beings fear them.*

pietrificato, pietrificata dalla paura
scared stiff, lit. petrified from fear
Pietrificato dalla paura, Matteo non ha più detto nulla.
Scared stiff, Matteo hasn't said a word since.

da brividi/panico/paura
frightening, creepy, lit. from shiver/panic/fear
Il ritorno in aereo fu da panico.
The flight back was frightening.

Laughter and Tears

piagnucolare
to whine; from *piangere*, to cry
Smettila di piagnucolare, Loredana! Il tuo ragazzo tornerà presto dall'America.
Stop whining, Loredana! Your boyfriend will come back soon from America.

piagnucolone, piagnucolona
whiner, lit. big whiner

Silvio, sei proprio un piagnucolone.
Silvio, you're such a whiner.

piangere il cuore a qualcuno

to break one's heart, lit. to make one's heart cry
Mi piange il cuore ogni volta che penso alla mia ex.
It breaks my heart every time I think about my ex.

faccia da funerale, f

sad face, lit. funeral face
Gioia, non fare questa faccia da funerale—vedrai che tutto andrà bene.
Sweetie, don't make that sad face—you'll see everything will be alright.

duro da mandare giù/da digerire

hard to swallow, lit. difficult to send down/difficult to digest
Quello che hai fatto alla mia migliore amica è proprio duro da digerire.
What you did to my best friend is really hard to swallow.

inghiottire il rospo

to eat crow, lit. to swallow the toad
Sua moglie lo ha lasciato ed ora deve inghiottire il rospo.
His wife left him and now he has to eat crow.

ridere di cuore

to have a hearty laugh, lit. to laugh from heart
Se avete riso di cuore al primo atto, il secondo vi farà scoppiare dal ridere.
If you had a hearty laugh during the first act, the second will make you laugh hysterically.

When people have fun, their limits often disappear. If you have to laugh, laugh openly—studies say it's healthy. Fare una risata a trentadue denti, *"making a laugh with thirty-two teeth," can hurt someone's ears, but will do you a lot of good. What can stop a good laugh? The laws of physics, dilatation, and elasticity.* Ridere a crepapelle, *"to laugh until the skin breaks," is used when laughing hysterically.* Pisciarsi addosso dalle risate, *"to pee oneself from laughter," is nearly the last state of laughing you want to experience . . . the next stage is* morire dal ridere, *"to die of laughter."*

il culo ride a qualcuno
to make someone laugh, lit. the ass laughs at someone
Mi ride il culo quando ripenso allo scherzo che ho fatto a Romano.
It makes me laugh when I think about the joke I played on Romano.

essere/andare in brodo di giuggiole (Veneto)
to be very happy, lit. to be in jujubes liquor
Quando le ho chiesto di sposarmi, Isabella é andata in un brodo di giuggiole.
When I asked her to marry me, Isabella was very happy.

essere al settimo cielo
to be in seventh heaven
Sono al settimo cielo perché sono stato promosso capo ufficio!
I'm in seventh heaven because I've been promoted to office manager!

Boredom and Fun

fare il muso a qualcuno
to be mad at someone, lit. to make the muzzle at someone
Posso sapere per quale motivo mi fai il muso?
Can I know why you're mad at me?

essere con le spalle al muro
to be up against a wall, lit. to be shoulders to the wall
A nessuno piace essere con le spalle al muro.
Nobody likes to be up against a wall.

essere giù di corda
to be down in the dumps, lit. to be down in the rope (boxing term)
Giulio è giù di corda da quando lui e sua moglie si sono lasciati.
Giulio has been down in the dumps since he and his wife split.

essere su di giri
to be in a good mood, lit. to be up in the turns
I risultati delle ultime elezioni mi hanno mandato su di giri.
The results of the last elections put me in a good mood.

arcistufo, arcistufa/stufissimo, stufissima
fed up, lit. very bored
I giocatori sono arcistufi del loro allenatore.
The players are fed up with their coach.

che figata
cool; from *figa*, pussy
Che figata, stasera andiamo a mangiarci una pizza tra amici.
Cool, tonight we're going to eat a pizza with friends.

seccatura, f

drag; from *seccare*, to dry
Che seccatura dovere lavorare il sabato.
What a drag to have to work on Saturdays.

seccare qualcuno

to annoy somebody, lit. to dry somebody
Il tuo amico ci sta seccando. Se ne deve andare.
Your friend is annoying us. He has to leave.

rottura di scatole/palle

ball breaker, lit. tin breaker/ball breaker
Che rottura di scatole! A Roma, dobbiamo aspettare cinque ore per la nostra coincidenza.
What a ballbreaker! In Rome, we have to wait five hours for our connection.

brontolone, brontolona

grouchy; from *brontolare*, to complain
Raffaele diventa sempre più brontolone.
Raffaele becomes grouchier and grouchier.

morire dalla noia

to die of boredom
Se non fosse per le discoteche, morirei dalla noia durante le vacanze.
If there weren't discotheques, I would die of boredom during vacation.

caspita!

wow!
Caspita, sei proprio fortunato Roberto.
Wow, you're really lucky Roberto.

rosso, rossa come un peperone

beet red, lit. as red as a pepper

Ornella gli ha dato un bacio sulla guancia, ed Edmondo è diventato rosso come un peperone.

Ornella gave Edmondo a kiss on the cheek, and he turned beet red.

Mood Swings

incazzato, incazzata/incavolato, incavolata (nero, nera/ come una iena)

pissed off; from *cazzo*, dick (black/like a hyena)

Incazzata come una iena, Diana è partita dal ristorante.

Pissed off, Diana left the restaurant.

mettere qualcuno alle corde/strette

to upset someone, lit. to put someone to the ropes/in narrow

Le lamentele di sua madre l'hanno messo alle strette ed ha lasciato la stanza.

His mother's complaints upset him and he left the room.

prendersela

to get upset, lit. to take it to oneself

Carmine se la prende per un nonnulla.

Carmine gets upset over nothing.

perdere le staffe

to freak out, to lose it, lit. to lose the stirrup

Leandro ha perso le staffe quando il suo vicino gli ha dato del figlio di puttana.

Leandro lost it when his neighbor called him a son of a bitch.

legarsi qualcosa al dito

to not forget something, lit. to tie something to the finger

Ken si è legato al dito il fatto che Marco gli è mancato di rispetto in pubblico.

Ken won't forget the fact that Marco made fun of him in public.

avere i nervi a fior di pelle

to have the jitters, lit. to have the nerves just under the skin

Da quando la ditta è stata venduta, tutti gli operai hanno i nervi a fior di pelle.

Since the company was sold, all the workers have had the jitters.

uscire dai gangheri

to go berserk, lit. to go out of the hinges

Il padrone ha chiesto a Debora di riscrivere la lettera ed è uscita dai gangheri.

The boss asked Debora to redo the letter and she went berserk.

saltare la mosca al naso a qualcuno

to get angry, lit. to jump the fly to someone's nose

A Miranda è saltata la mosca al naso quando Elisa le ha detto che era una stupida.

Miranda got angry when Elisa called her a dummy.

con la luna storta

in a bad mood, lit. with the twisted moon

Fabrizio si è svegliato con la luna storta.

Fabrizio woke up in a bad mood.

avere un diavolo per capello

to be very upset, lit. to have a devil for hair

Lasciamo Kevin in pace. Oggi ha un diavolo per capello!

Let's leave Kevin in peace. Today he's very upset!

avercela con qualcuno

to be mad at someone, lit. to have it against someone

Se ce l'hai con me, dimmelo!

If you're mad at me, tell me!

elettrizzato, elettrizzata

excited, lit. electrified

Simonetta, la secchiona della classe, è tutta elettrizzata perché è stata invitata ad una festa.

Simonetta, the class nerd, is all excited because she's been invited to a party.

farsi una camomilla

to keep quiet, to cool down, lit. make oneself a chamomile

Fatti una camomilla, sennò ti viene un infarto.

Cool down, or you'll have a stroke.

Surprise

va che roba!

wow, lit. what a stuff

Va che roba, un laptop di seconda mano con tutti i software per solo cento euro!

Wow, a secondhand laptop with all the software for only one hundred euro!

rimanere a bocca aperta

to be flabbergasted, lit. to stay open mouthed

Quando Camilla si è spogliata, Giordano è rimasto a bocca aperta.

When Camilla took off her clothes, Giordano was flabbergasted.

ammazza!
wow!, lit. kill!
Ammazza, che bona la commessa!
Wow, the cashier is a hottie!

bestiale
cool, amazing, lit. beastly
'Sto videogioco è troppo bestiale!
This videogame is so cool!

ostia
hey, lit. *ostie*
Ostia, oggi e il tuo compleanno!
Hey, today's your birthday!

CHAPTER NINE

Farsi un culo così:

Yes, You Do Need an Education

Though it pretends to be united, Italy is a divided nation. Like the American southerners in the Civil War, many northern Italians would like to secede. While *Roma* is the capital, the northern city of *Milano* is the economic heart of Italy, where work opportunities are found and to which many immigrants are drawn. The south, by contrast, is mostly agricultural, and young people tend to continue their studies (there are very few work opportunities); whereas up north, kids go to work immediately after school.

Italy is a very entrepreneurial country, considered by many immigrants to be the European version of the United States. People come from northern Africa and the rest of the developing world to get a piece of this American—sorry—Italian dream. This is quite funny, considering it has been several decades since Italy was truly an economic leader. In the fifties and sixties, after World War II, Italy was one of Europe's powerhouses. Italy had an economic boom when protectionism was lifted, revitalizing industries nationwide. But sadly those golden years are gone, as industries have shifted production to cheaper areas in Eastern Europe and the far East. Now unemployment runs high, government scandals have dismayed the public, and not even the experts are sure when or if Italy will come out of its slump.

School

biblio, f
library, abbr. of *biblioteca*, library
Passa tutto il tempo libero alla biblio.
She spends all her free time at the library.

topo di biblioteca, m
bookworm, lit. library mouse
Martina, 'sto topo di biblioteca, potrebbe leggere libri dalla mattina alla sera . . .
Martina, that bookworm, could read books from morning 'til night . . .

caserma, f
school, lit. barracks
Oggi, per via del caldo, hanno chiuso la caserma.
Today, because of the heat, they closed the school.

For a lot of children, school is synonymous with the end of freedom, inhumanity, confinement, and forced labor. Which word is better to express those conditions than Lager, the German word for "concentration camp"? The same aspects are present in la galera, "jail," but il manicomio, "mental institution," sheds light on how crazy kids think school is.

prof, m, f

teacher, abbr. of *professore*, professor

La prof di tedesco ci fa paura!

The German teacher scares us!

secchione, secchiona

enthusiastic student, nerd, lit. big bucket

I secchioni sono amati dai prof ed odiati dagli studenti.

Nerds are loved by teachers and hated by students.

studiare la lezione a pappagallo

to learn by heart, lit. to study the lesson the parrot way

Invece di studiare la lezione a pappagallo, perché non provi a capirne il contenuto?

Instead of learning the lesson by heart, why don't you try to understand its content?

essere una bestia in qualcosa

to be very talented in/at something, lit. to be a beast in something

Melissa è una bestia negli affari.

Melissa is very talented in business.

mate, f

math, abbr. of *matematica*, mathematics

Maria non ha ancora dato l'esame di mate.

Maria hasn't yet passed the math examination.

fare chiodo a scuola

to play hookie, lit. to make nail at school

Ogni volta che Dylan lo poteva, faceva chiodo a scuola.

Every time Dylan could do it, he played hookie.

Mathematics, history, foreign languages, and literature may inspire some students, but for many (funny enough this only happens in countries where education is an accessible right) other activities are preferred. If children play hookie in the States, in Italy they will marinare la scuola, *"marinate the school,"* or segare, *"saw." If the school tries to straighten out the students, some will resist and decide to* bigiare la scuola *(Nord), from the German* biegen, *"to bend the school."*

barare
to cheat
Con questo professore è impossibile barare!
It's impossible to cheat with this teacher!

sgamare
to catch
Il prof di spagnolo ha sgamato Igor mentre fumava.
The Spanish teacher caught Igor smoking.

spremersi le meningi
to rack one's brain, lit. to squeeze one's brain
Per riuscire quel problema dovrete spremervi le meningi.
In order to solve that problem you'll have to rack your brain.

scervellarsi
to pick one's brain; from *cervello*, brain
Si sono scervellati per ore senza trovare la soluzione.
They picked their brains for hours without finding the solution.

grattacapo, m
brainteaser, lit. that itches the head

Il prof di mate ci ha dato un nuovo grattacapo da risolvere.
The math teacher gave us a new brainteaser to solve.

mattone, m
hard, lit. brick
Il test di chimica non mi è sembrato un mattone.
The chemistry test didn't look so hard to me.

essere una passeggiata
to be a cinch, lit. to be a stroll
L'esame di filosofia era una passeggiata.
The philosophy exam was a cinch.

buffonata, f
easy task; from *buffone*, buffoon
Rimediare al presunto bug informatico del 2000 si è avverato essere una buffonata.
Solving the supposed 2000 computer bug happened to be an easy task.

menata/rottura/palla, f
pain in the ass; from *menare*, lead/break/ball
Riempire le pratiche d'ammissione è sempre una menata.
To fill out an admission form is always a pain in the ass.

Workers and Work

marocchino, marocchina
street vendor, lit. Moroccan
Quando ha visto il poliziotto, il marocchino ha preso la sua roba ed è scappato.
As soon as the street vendor saw the policeman, he packed his merchandise and ran away.

beccamorto, m

undertaker, lit. one who catches the dead ones

I beccamorti hanno pochi amici.

Undertakers have few friends.

tosacani/tosapecore, m

men's/women's hairdresser, lit. one who shears dogs/sheep

Dovresti cambiare tosacani. 'Sto taglio fa schifo!

You should change hairdressers. That haircut sucks!

bocia, f

recruit; from *boccia*, ball

Tagliano i capelli delle bocie molto corti.

They cut the recruits' hair very short.

mezza manica, f/scribacchino, scribacchina

bad writer, lit. half sleeve/little scribe

Si prende per il nuovo Manzoni, ma rimane uno scribacchino.

He pretends he's the new Manzoni, but he's only a bad writer.

avere anni di qualcosa alle spalle

to have years of experience in something, lit. to have years of something behind the shoulders

Dagli retta per quel che riguarda la scelta del software. Marco ha anni d'informatica alle spalle.

Listen to what he says about the choice of software. Marco has years of experience in IT.

fare un lavoro con i piedi/da cani/di merda

to do a shitty job, lit. to do work with the feet/the dog way/of shit

La ditta di costruzioni che ho assunta ha fatto un lavoro da cani.

The construction company I hired did a shitty job.

fare un lavoro a coppola di minchia
to do shitty work, lit. to do a job at cap of dicks
La ditta edilizia ha fatto un lavoro a coppola di minchia.
The construction company did shitty work.

mettercela tutta
to go all out, lit. to put all in it
Se ce la mettiamo tutta, ragazzi, ce la faremo in due ore.
If we go all out, guys, we'll finish it in two hours.

olio di gomito, m
elbow grease
Ci servirà un po' di olio di gomito per pulire questa vecchia vasca da bagno.
We'll need a little elbow grease to clean this old bathtub.

sfacchinata, f
heavy work; from *facchino*, porter
Posare le travi sul tetto è stata una vera facchinata.
Placing the beams on the roof was real heavy work.

farsi un culo così
to work one's ass off, lit. to make oneself an ass like that
Gli agricoltori si fanno un culo così, ma guadagnano poco.
Farmers work their asses off, but earn very little.

farsi un mazzo
to work very hard, lit. to make oneself a cluster
Gli architetti si sono fatti un mazzo per presentare il progetto in tempo.
The architects worked very hard to present the project on time.

Most people agree that work is healthy and sloth is bad. Popular expressions, though, give a completely different point of view. Working hard causes huge pain, even a pain in the ass. Some italiani *may ask themselves why they should* spaccarsi il culo, *"break their ass," for their boss. Deformations of the body occur in* farsi un culo grosso così, *"to get oneself an ass big like that," as well as* sgobbare, *"to slog, to work hard," "to become hunchback." The inhumanity of working reveals itself in* lavorare come una bestia, *"to work like a beast" . . . and you wonder where the Italians get their reputation for being lazy!*

andare allo sgobbo

to go to work; from *gobbo*, hunchback
Ogni lunedì mattina, nessuno vuole andare allo sgobbo.
On Monday morning, no one wants to go to work.

staccare

to finish work, lit. to unplug
Venerdì stacco prima e ti vengo a prendere.
Friday I'll finish work earlier and I'll come get you.

gettare la spugna

to throw in the towel, lit. to throw the sponge
È ora di gettare la spugna; la partita è persa.
It's time to throw in the towel; the game is lost.

mandare in fumo/a monte/in vacca

to spoil, lit. to send in smoke/to the mount/in cow
Due settimane prima del suo matrimonio, Battista ha mandato tutto a monte.
Two weeks before his wedding, Battista spoiled everything.

buttare qualcosa all'aria

to say to hell with something, lit. to send something in the air

Mauro ha buttato tutto all'aria ed è entrato in un setta satanica.

Mauro said to hell with everything and joined a satanic cult.

mollare la baracca

to quit, lit. to let the shack go

Obama ha mollato la baracca un mese prima che la società fallisse.

Obama quit his job one month before the company folded.

buttare fuori

to fire/throw out

Il boss lo ha buttato fuori.

The boss threw him out.

cacciare via

to fire, lit. to chase away

Patrizia non sarà mai cacciata via dall'ufficio.

Patrizia will never get fired from the office.

scansafatiche, m, f

lazybones, lit. one who puts aside the fatigues

Omar non vuole lavorare perché è uno scansafatiche.

Omar doesn't want to work because he's a lazybones.

Italy desperately needs workers for its agriculture in the South and industries in the North. Il lavoro all'italiana, work the Italian way, may be part of the reason. If you get to see some outdoor workers, pay attention; there's usually one guy working and two (sometimes up to three) people watching him. So once again Italy

*is divided in two: on one side are the hard workers
and their masochistic attitude toward work. On the
other are those who have developed all kinds of
alternative activities to work:* i fannulloni, *literally
"the ones who do nothing," also called* i pigroni, *"the
lazy ones" and* i perdigiorno, *literally "the ones who
lose their day."*

grattarsi la pancia
to twiddle one's thumbs, lit. to scratch one's stomach
**I neo pensionati si grattano la pancia, mentre gli
ex-colleghi li invidiano.**
*The new retirees twiddle their thumbs, while their ex-colleagues
envy them.*

rigirarsi i pollici
to do nothing, lit. to roll over the thumbs
Dorotea si rigira i pollici mentre suo marito lavora sodo.
Dorotea does nothing while her husband works hard.

*What can a worker do, especially if he was a hard-
worker, once he's retired? Activities are not so varied
and interesting and many retirees* stanno con le mani
in mano, *"twiddle their thumbs." Other lazy activities
are more likely to give pleasure:* cazzeggiare/non fare
un cazzo, *literally "to not make a dick," and the most
vulgar one,* grattarsi le palle, *"to scratch one's balls."
Inactivity is indeed* la madre del vizio, *"the mother of
all vices."*

battere la fiacca

to run out of energy, lit. to beat the drowsiness

Forza ragazzi! Non battete la fiacca! È questo il meglio che sapete dare?

Come on guys! Don't run out of energy! Is this the best you can do?

CHAPTER TEN

Ricco sfondato:

Shake Your Moneymaker

While most of Italy is solidly middle or working class, the gap between rich and poor seems to be widening. Nowhere is this more evident than in the geographic split between north and south. *Milano*, the economic capital of Italy and the siege of *la borsa*, the stock market, lies far north. The surrounding states, *Lombardia*, *Veneto*, and *Piemonte*, are the most prosperous in Italy. This region, known as *la pianura Padana*, often talks of succession from *la repubblica* in order to keep profits from their strong economy closer to home.

But what to do with this wealth and how to hide it rather than paying taxes which will go directly to Rome? Fiscal havens, such as *il Principato di Monaco* to the west and Switzerland to the north have traditionally been and are still today excellent places for concealing money. In the case of Switzerland (the only other European country where Italian is a national language), the previously sleepy, lakeside city of Lugano now boasts only banks and chic hotels for wealthy Italians.

Money and People

grana, f
dough, lit. grain
Ridammi la grana o ti picchio!
Give me the dough back or I'll kick you!

peculio, m
savings; from *pecora*, sheep
In trenta anni di lavoro, Guglielmo si è messo da parte un grosso peculio.
After thirty years of working, Guglielmo put aside a lot of savings.

mucchio di soldi, m
pile of money, lit. pile of money
Con una buona idea e un capitale iniziale, faremo un mucchio di soldi.
With a good idea and initial capital, we'll make a pile of money.

sacco di quattrini, m
loads of cash, lit. a bag of coins
Marco e Gregory si fanno un sacco di quattrini vendendo azioni.
Marco and Gregory made loads of cash selling stocks.

scegliere a testa o croce
to flip a coin, lit. to choose by head or cross
I due amici hanno scelto a testa o croce chi sarebbe uscito con Valeria.
The two friends flipped a coin to see who would go out with Valeria.

pidocchio, pidocchia

stingy, lit. lice

Non fare il pidocchio; per favore, offrici un gelato!

Don't be stingy; treat us to an ice cream, please!

Words may change from country to country or region to region, but stinginess is universal: hence tirchio, spilorcio, *and* taccagno *are common insults. Expressions like* una persona di manica stretta, *or* una persona che ha il braccino corto, *"a person with short sleeves" or "with a short arm," can't reach the wallet in his/her back pocket.* Avere ragnatelle nel portafoglio, *"to have spider webs in the wallet," is used to describe people who rarely open their wallets. Racism, pure and simple, is the reason some Italians may refer to Jews negatively regarding money. As a result you may hear someone called* un rabbino, *"rabbi,"* un israelita, *"Israelite," or* un Abramuccio, *"a little Abraham," when counting his money.* Lo scozzese, *the Scottish, and* il Genovese, *Genoans, share the same derogative connotation. Other words for avarice include* pidocchieria, *from* pidocchio, *"lice,"* taccagneria, tirchieria, *and* spilorceria.

granoso, granosa

loaded; from *grano, grana*, grain

Le vecchie granose si riconoscono subito. Tengono la borsa vicinissimo al corpo.

Loaded old ladies are easy to recognize. They keep their purses close to their body.

buon partito, m

rich husband, lit. good part

Le sorelle Rossi si cercano ni buoni partiti.

The Rossi sisters are looking for rich husbands.

nuotare nell'oro

to be rolling in dough, lit. to swim in gold

Non avrei mai pensato che la vecchietta della porta accanto nuotasse nell'oro.

I would never have thought that the old lady next door was rolling in dough.

ricco sfondato, ricca sfondata

to be obscenely rich, lit. to be bottomless rich

Se fossi ricco sfondato come te, regalerei soldi ai miei migliori amici.

If I were as obscenely rich as you, I'd give some money to my best friends.

People make use of suffixes and prefixes, expressions, and all kind of images to give the idea of those huge ricchezze. Ricco come il maiale, *"rich as a pig,"* ricchissimo, straricco, *"over-rich,"* riccone, *"big rich,"* and essere imbottito di banconote, *"to be stuffed with paper money,"* all target the same "poor" victims—the rich!

---

nascere con la camicia

to be born with a silver spoon in one's mouth, lit. to be born with the shirt

Carlotta è nata con la camicia. Da bambina ha avuto tutto quello che voleva.

Carlotta was born with a silver spoon in her mouth. As a child she had everything she wanted.

vivere come un pascià

to live like a king, lit. to live like a pasha

Certo lo stipendio non ti permette di vivere come un pascià, ma non significa nemmeno che devi vivere come un morto di fame.

Of course your salary doesn't allow you to live like a king, but it doesn't mean you have to live like you're dying of hunger either.

figlio, figlia di papà

rich kid, lit. daddy's boy, daddy's girl

I figli di papà tendano a pensare e vestire nello stesso modo.

Rich kids tend to think and dress alike.

"Daddy's kids" were originally given the name of the place they tended to meet up. These names change depending on the city involved. In Torino, *they're called* cabinotti, *from* la cabina telefonica, *"public phone booth."* Bolognesi *call them* fighetti, *"cute ones," from the expensive clothes they wear. The ritzy area of Rome,* Parioli, *gave its youth the name* Pariolini, *while Genoa has its own* Albarini, *from* Albaro. *Even the famous Catholic school San Carlo in Milan has a nickname for the youngsters who study there,* i Sancarlini.

essere della (insert name of city) bene

to be rich

Non sapevo che fossi della Roma bene!
I didn't know you were a rich Roman!

vivere nei quartieri alti/bassi

to be rich/poor, lit. to live in the high/low quarters
Non mi avevi detto che Monica viveva nei quartieri bassi.
You didn't tell me that Monica was poor.

morto, morta di fame

dying of hunger, lit. dead of hunger
Non pensare che siamo morti di fame; siamo solo un po'spilorci.
Don't think we are dying of hunger; we're just a bit stingy.

tutto fumo e niente arrosto

all talk, lit. all smoke and no roast
Non mi lascio ingannare; penso che quell'agente immobiliare sia tutto fumo e niente arrosto.
Nobody can fool me; I think this real estate agent is all talk.

vivere a scrocco di qualcuno

to sponge off someone; from *scrocco*, scrounge
John ha trent'anni e vive a scrocco dei suoi genitori.
John is thirty and sponges off his parents.

vivere sulle spalle degli altri

to live on someone else's dime, lit. to live on others' shoulders
Non penso che potrai vivere in eterno sulle spalle degli altri.
I don't think you'll be able to live on someone else's dime forever.

poveraccio, poveraccia

poor guy, poor girl; from *povero*, poor with the *-accio* suffix
Che poveracci, nessuno vorrebbe essere al loro posto.
Poor guys, no one would like to be in their place.

barbone, barbona

homeless person, bum, lit. big-bearded one

Jason ha vissuto nel lusso prima di finire barbone.

Jason lived in luxury before he ended up as a bum.

a caval' donato (non si guarda in bocca)

beggars can't be choosers, don't look a gift horse in the mouth, lit. (don't look in the mouth) of a given horse

La casa di vacanza che ci ha prestato Alberto non è il massimo, ma a caval' donato non si guarda in bocca.

The vacation house offered by Alberto is not the nicest, but beggars can't be choosers.

finire in mezzo alla strada

to end up in the streets

Se la nostra ditta non ottiene l'appalto comunale, tutti noi finiremmo in mezzo alla strada.

If our company doesn't win the tender, we'll all end up in the streets.

senza una lira

penniless, lit. without a *lira*, former Italian currency

Il suo ragazzo ha giocato a poker tutta la notte ed è tornato senza una lira a casa.

Her boyfriend played poker all night long and came back home penniless.

avere le tasche vuote/finire a tasche vuote

to be broke, lit. to have empty pockets/end up with empty pockets

Ti aiuterei con piacere ma ho le tasche vuote.

I'd gladly help you but I'm broke too.

Being broke is like being rich: you don't necessary want people to know it. Instead of using the words "poor," "broke," or "penniless," Italians prefer to employ essere al verde, *"to be in the green,"* essere in (banca)rotta, *"to be in bankruptcy,"* essere in bolletta, *literally "to be in bill."* Avere le pezze al culo, *literally "to have patches on the ass," is reserved for people who don't have enough money to buy new clothes when their old ones are ripped. Instead, they'll sew on patches and wear these clothes again and again.*

fare la fame
to be broke, lit. to starve
Da quando ha perso il lavoro in banca, Marina fa la fame.
Since she lost her job at the bank, Marina is broke.

Saving, Making, and Losing Money

pagare sull'unghia
to pay cash, lit. to pay on the nail
Se ti pago sull'unghia, mi fai uno sconto?
If I pay you cash, will you give me a discount?

avere le mani/tasche bucate
to have holes in one's pockets, lit. to have holes in hand/pockets with holes
Non puoi dargli più di cento euro, o li spenderà tutti in slot machines. Ha le mani bucate.
Don't give him more than a hundred euro, or he'll spend it all in slot machines. He has holes in his pockets.

rimanere a secco

to be cleaned out, lit. to stay dry

Siamo rimasti a secco dopo aver giocato al casinò.

We were cleaned out after we played at the casino.

sganciare/scucire i soldi

to spit out the money, lit. to unhook/unpick the money

Avete perso la scommessa, allora sganciate i soldi adesso.

You lost the bet, so spit out the money now.

costare un occhio della testa/un patrimonio/una cifra

to cost an arm and a leg, lit. to cost one eye of the head/a patrimony

La chirurgia plastica costa un patrimonio, ma nel tuo caso sarà un buon investimento.

Plastic surgery costs an arm and a leg, but in your case it would be a good investment.

sbarcare il lunario

to make ends meet, lit. to disembark the lunar calendar

Nicola non riesce a sbarcare il lunario e non vuole che l'aiuti.

Nicola can't make ends meet and doesn't want me to help him.

affarone, m

bargain, good deal, lit. big bargain

Non lasciatevi rubare quell'affarone!

Don't let that bargain get away!

successone, m

big hit, lit. big success

Il prossimo film di questo regista sarà un successone.

This director's next movie is going to be a big hit.

fare soldi a palate

to make a lot of money

Anche quando l'economia va male, c'è sempre chi si fa soldi a palate.

Even when the economy is going badly, there will always be people who make a lot of money.

buco, m

deficit, lit. hole

L'impresa ha nascosto a tutti il buco.

The company hid the deficit from everyone.

stringere/tirare la cinghia

to cut expenses, lit. to tighten/pull the belt

Ci toccherà stringere la cinghia se vogliamo sbarcare il lunario.

We'll have to cut expenses if we want to make ends meet.

pagare alla romana

to go Dutch, lit. to pay the Roman way

Gli amici di solito pagano alla romana.

Friends usually go Dutch.

fisarmonica, f

wallet, lit. accordion

Dario ha lasciato la fisarmonica sul tavolo del ristorante. Due minuti dopo era sparita.

Dario left his wallet on the table at the restaurant. Two minutes later it disappeared.

93

CHAPTER ELEVEN

Guardia o ladro:

The Wrong Side of the Law

Creata la legge, creato l'inganno, lit. "create the law, create the swindle," isn't a national motto, but certainly could be. It seems the Mafia has taken over much of Italy, especially the bottom half of the boot. People rich or poor are often considered potential criminals or con men, and working under the table, extracting money from the Italian IRS, and screwing over business partners has become an art form. This problem isn't just for the lower classes—it is present in every layer of society, from the *pomodoro* farmer to the politician.

Italy loves a good scandal: abusive agricultural subsidies, poisoned *panettone*, traditional blackmail, and fixed soccer games all thrill the general public. Also known as *Cosa nostra*, *la Camorra* (in Naples), *la 'Ndrangheta* (in Calabria), the Mafia keeps busy with illegal schemes throughout the country. No scheme is too small to bother with. Take for example Italy's absurdly high blindness rate—sadly, one of the easiest disabilities to fake. And you'd think from the outrageous number of work-related disabilities that most Italians work as firemen or Formula One drivers.

giallo, m
thriller, lit. yellow
Nadia legge solo gialli.
Nadia reads only thrillers.

Choosing One's Team

pola/madama/signora, f
cop, abbr. of *polizia*, police, lit. madame, lady
Dopo la rapina, la pola ha interrogato tutto il vicinato.
After the robbery, the police interrogated the entire neighborhood.

celerino, m
cop, lit. the fast one
I tifosi hanno picchiato a morte un celerino.
The fans beat a cop to death.

sbirro, m (rosbi in Verlan)
cop; from *birro*, medieval word for policeman
Giulio lavora per gli sbirri.
Giulio works for the cops.

polino, m
cop, abbr. of *polizia* with *-ino* suffix, used for cops on motorcycles
Il polino ha fermato il motociclista perché non portava il casco.
The cop stopped the motorcyclist because he wasn't wearing a helmet.

piedipiatti, m
cop, lit. flat feet

I piedipiatti hanno circondato la casa dei ladri.
The cops encircled the thieves' house.

caramba, m

state police, from *carabinieri*
I caramba sono quasi tutti meridionali.
The state police are almost all Southerners.

Carabinieri, *the Italian national police, are barely respected by the general public. They're especially targeted in the north due to their southern origins. To become national policemen, candidates must take several national tests, which only the most educated and skilled applicants pass. There's no such thing as a test like those to become* un poliziotto *or regular policeman. Despite their high IQs,* carabinieri *are seen as stupid; northerners make fun of everything including their southern accents. They're often called* caramba *or* questurini, *from* la questura, *"police station."*

fiamme gialle, fpl

financial cops, lit. yellow flames, the shield of the *guardia di finanza*
Le fiamme gialle hanno investigato diversi imprenditori locali.
The financial cops investigated different local entrepreneurs.

scafista, m

smuggler (sea), abbr. of *motoscafista*, speedboat driver
Per non farsi prendere, gli scafisti hanno buttato i loro passeggeri in mare.
In order not to get caught, the smugglers threw their passengers in the sea.

mafioso, m
Mobster, lit. one who works for the Mafia
I mafiosi sono molto discreti.
Mobsters are very discreet.

COSA NOSTRA:
The Mafia holds an incredible attraction for many Americans. It is the subject of countless Hollywood films and legends, but in reality is no laughing matter. Both the Mafia and the Italian state fight for control of the masses. When officials investigate, they are conveniently killed in explosions, like Borsellino and Falcone, the famous judges ruling on Mafia cases. Sicily in particular has no clear distinction between people in power and *Mafiosi*. Decades of attempting to disable the Mafia have had little to no effect. While these years of *inchieste* led to the arrest of a Godfather, the body of the criminal organization kept on breathing. But a change may come soon. Some *commercianti* and *imprenditori* have created the association *Addiopizzo*, literally "goodbye pizzo," the tax or protection fee paid to *la cosa nostra*. If other shopkeepers and merchants do the same, or if customers opt to use only these "clean" businesses, the idea of the ever-present Mafia ingrained in the minds of so many Italians may eventually disappear.

pentito, m
ex-mafia boss, lit. repentant
Il pentito ha dato preziose informazioni in cambio della sua libertà.
The ex-Mafia boss gave precious information in exchange for his freedom.

talpa, f
mole

I servizi segreti hanno talpe in tutti i gruppuscoli terroristici.
Secret services have moles in all terrorist cells.

pezzo grosso, m
big shot, lit. big piece
I pezzi grossi non si fanno mai prendere.
Big shots never get caught.

malandrino, m
crook
Il nostro tassista era un bel malandrino. La corsa c'è costata una cifra enorme!
Our Neapolitan taxi driver was a real crook. The ride cost us an arm and a leg!

farabutto/canaglia
rascal
Quel farabutto di Cesare, se n'è andato senza pagare.
Cesare, that rascal, left without paying.

essere pulito, pulita
to be clean
Ti puoi fidare di Leila, è pulita.
You can trust Leila, she's clean.

bidonista, m
swindler, trickster, lit. one who makes barrels/swindles
Per fare il bidonista uno deve essere molto furbo.
To become a swindler one has to be very clever.

ballista, m
bullshitter, lit. who tells balls

Che ballista tuo fratello!
What a bullshitter your brother is!

ladruncolo, ladruncola
thief; from *ladro*, thief with the *-uncolo* suffix
Cristina era una ladruncola ma adesso è una perfetta casalinga.
Cristina was a thief, but now she's the perfect housewife.

The Game

scippo, f
purse snatching, lit. from *scippare*, to steal
Gli scippi abbondano nelle metropoli italiane.
Purse snatchings are frequent in Italian cities.

rubare
to steal, abbr. of *derubare*, to steal
Tieni d'occhi questi giovanotti; rubano di tutto per sfida.
Keep an eye on these young guys; they steal everything for laughs.

avere le mani lunghe
to be a thief, to steal, lit. to have long hands
State attenti ai bambini nelle stazioni; hanno le mani lunghe.
Be careful of the children at train stations; they're thieves.

Italy suffers from a bad reputation: pickpockets and petty criminals abound. You'll see people carrying their car stereos to prevent thieves from stealing them. Il motorino and la Vespa are used to scippare old ladies'

purses. Bands of teenagers (often the unprivileged chil-
dren of poor immigrants) are casually waiting to empty
tourists' pockets before the taxi drivers beat them to it.
The vocabulary, but not the motive, changes from region
to region: derubare *becomes* fregare, azzottare *(Roma),*
imboscare, *literally "to hide in a forest." Enjoy your stay*
but keep an eye on your stuff.

imboscata, f

trap; from *bosco*, wood, forest
La polizia ha preparato un'imboscata.
The police prepared a trap.

fare un colpo grosso

to pull a big job, lit. to do a big/fat kick
**Nessuno sa che dei ladri stanno per fare un colpo grosso
al casinò.**
Nobody knows thieves are about to pull a big job at the casino.

fare fuori/secco qualcuno

to rub someone out, lit. to make someone out/dry
Il teste è stato fatto secco dagli amici dell'imputato.
The witness was rubbed out by the accused's friends.

bidonare qualcuno

to cheat, swindle someone; from *bidone*, barrel
**Carmine e Giuliana si sono fatti bidonare da un agente
immobiliare.**
Carmine and Giuliana were swindled by a real estate agent.

bidonata/bidone, m

swindle, trick

Sono tanti gli anziani a cascare nel bidone "del nipote Tedesco."
Many old folks fell for the "German nephew swindle."

cascare/cascarci
to be duped, lit. to fall (in it)
Era un bidone e tu ci sei cascato.
It was a trick and you got duped.

bustarella/tangente, f
bribe, lit. little envelope/tangent
Il sindaco ha ricevuto una bustarella dalla ditta di costruzioni.
The mayor received a bribe from the construction company.

tangentopoli, f
bribery, lit. city of bribery
Il giudice Di Pietro lottava contro tangentopoli.
The judge Di Pietro fought against bribery.

During the first Berlusconi government in the 1980s, Judge Di Pietro revealed the bribery of funzionari di stato, *politicians, and* eletti. Le tangenti *were given by big industrial and media lobbies as well as construction companies in exchange for expensive national project contracts. Di Pietro's "clean hands" effort,* mani pulite, *had some success but was unable to snag the big fish. Disgusted, but now popular thanks to his* mastro lindo—*Mr. Clean image—Di Pietro quit his job to pursue political aspirations.*

taroccato, taroccata
fake, counterfeit; maybe from *tarocchi*, tarot cards

Vanessa ha comprato profumi taroccati durante il suo viaggio in Russia.
Vanessa bought counterfeit perfume during her trip to Russia.

venire a galla/alla luce del sole

to come to light, lit. to come on the surface of the water/to the sun light

Prima o poi la verità verrà alla luce del sole.
Sooner or later the truth will come to light.

ficcarsi nei guai

to get oneself in hot water, lit. to put oneself inside problems
Claudio si ficca sempre nei guai.
Claudio always gets himself in hot water.

esserci dentro fino al collo

to be up shit's creek, lit. to be inside it/in shit up to the neck
Ragazzi, se non facciamo qualcosa subito ci saremo dentro fino al collo.
Guys, if we don't do something quickly we'll be up shit's creek.

pasticcio, m

mess; from *pasticceria*, bakery
Hai fatto un bel pasticcio; era meglio se non mi aiutavi.
You made a big mess; it would have been better if you hadn't helped me.

End of Game

perquisa, f

search (police), abbr. of *perquisizione*
La perquisa è stata inutile.
The search was in vain.

dare la caccia a qualcuno

to chase someone, lit. to give the hunting to someone

La guardacoste dà la caccia ai motoscafi albanesi.

The coast guard chases Albanian speedboats.

tagliare la corda

to run away, lit. to cut the rope

I ladri hanno tagliato la corda dopo avere svuotato la cassaforte.

The thieves ran away after they emptied the safe.

darsela a gambe (levate)

to run away, lit. to give it to oneself to legs (in the air)

Quando arriva la polizia, i clandestini se la danno a gambe levate.

When the police come, illegal immigrants run away.

inchiodare qualcuno

to nail someone

I carabinieri non hanno ancora inchiodato i rapinatori della banca.

The gendarmes haven't nailed the bank robbers.

beccare

to catch; from *becco*, beak, lit. to hit/take with the beak

Non beccheranno mai il cervello della banda.

They'll never catch the ringleader.

pinzare/pizzicare

to catch, lit. to pinch

Dopo anni d'inchiesta, la polizia ha pinzato il boss mafioso.

After years of enquiries, the police caught the Mafia boss.

essere colto sul fatto/con le mani nel sacco/in castagna

to be caught red-handed, lit. to pick someone in the fact/with the hands in the purse/ in chestnut

Il ladro è stato colto in castagna.

The thief was caught red-handed.

sbattere dentro

to send to jail, lit. to throw/bang inside

Se ti prende la polizia, ti sbatte dentro di sicuro.

If the police catch you, they'll send you to jail for sure.

in gabbia/al fresco

in jail, lit. caged/outside

Il mio papà è rimasto dieci anni in gabbia per aggressione.

My dad spent ten years in jail for assault.

CHAPTER TWELVE

Un medico in famiglia:

Following Doctors' Orders

Italians have a special relationship with medicine and doctors. As Italy is a very Catholic country, Italians generally recognize only one savior and he isn't likely to be found in a hospital. One need go no further than reading some local sayings to better understand just how Italians feel about this topic.

Medici e guerre spopolano le terre. Doctors and wars depopulate the Earth.

I falli del dottore li copre la terra. Doctor's mistakes are covered by dirt.

Italian health care is both good and bad. On the one hand, every cent spent on health care is picked up by *la mutua*, the Italian health care system. On the other hand, there are long waiting lists for transplantation, as well as bribery and unequal treatment (the rich can pay private doctors for immediate, lifesaving treatment). In summer 2007, a popular TV show revealed the actual state of Italian hospitals. When looking in the basements of the supposedly cleanest and safest places, the reporters found particles of asbestos falling from insulation material as well as medical garbage and rats as big as cats! Be assured, however, in case you have the misfortune to require a hospital visit while vacationing: Italian medical care itself is excellent. Just be sure to check for rat poop in your IV.

People and Places

strizzacervelli, m
shrink, lit. who squeezes the brains
Dopo lo stupro, la giovane vittima ha dovuto andare dallo strizzacervelli.
After the rape, the young victim had to go to see a shrink.

macellaio, m
butcher, bad surgeon
Non voglio finire nelle mani di quel macellaio.
I don't want to wind up in the hands of that butcher.

fabbrica di angioletti, f
abortion clinic, lit. little angels factory
I cattolici italiani vogliono chiudere le fabbriche di angioletti.
Italian Catholics want to close abortion clinics.

finire in sala operatoria
to end up in the operating room
Stefano ha rotto un legamento ed è finito in sala operatoria.
Stefano tore a ligament and ended up in the operating room.

Shape and Problems

impiastrarsi
to crash into; from *impiastro*, disastrous person

Il giovane autista si è impiastrato contro un albero.
The inexperienced driver crashed into a tree.

schiantato, schiantata
severely injured
Fausto si è schiantato con la macchina.
Fausto was severely injured in a car accident.

scassato, scassata
wrecked
Giorgio è tornato dalle sue vacanze tutto scassato.
Giorgio came back from his holidays completely wrecked.

a pezzi
broken, lit. in pieces
Melissa era a pezzi quando le hanno detto che sua madre era morta.
Melissa was broken when they told her her mother was dead.

cadere in depressione
to fall into a depression
I suoi genitori sono caduti in depressione dopo aver perso tutti i risparmi.
His parents fell into a depression after they lost all their savings.

essere distrutto
to be dead tired, lit. to be destroyed
Sono distrutto. Non ce la faccio più!
I'm dead tired. I can't take anymore!

stanco morto, stanca morta
dead tired
Stanchi morti, sono andati subito a letto.
Dead tired, they went straight to bed.

avere una brutta cera

to look terrible, lit. to have a bad wax

Mamma mia, hai un brutta cera Carmela. Ti sei ammalata?

Oh my God, you look terrible Carmela. Are you sick?

fuso, fusa

burnt out, lit. melted, fused

Dopo aver lavorato come un pazzo per anni, Pietro era del tutto fuso.

After working like a dog for years, Pietro was completely burnt out.

(idea) fissa, f

fixed idea

Emilio non sopportava più le fisse della sua partner sulla fedeltà e l'ha lasciata.

Emilio couldn't take his partner's fixed ideas about fidelity anymore and he dumped her.

chiodo fisso, m

obsession, lit. fixed nail

Il chiodo fisso di Alessio è di diventare pilota di Formula Uno.

Alessio's obsession is to become a Formula One racer.

Recovery and Healing

farcela

to get over it, lit. to make it

Ce la farai, Maria.

You'll get over it, Maria.

tenere duro

to hang in there, lit. to keep hard

Tieni duro, il peggio è alle spalle.

Hang in there, the worst is over.

correre un rischio

to run the risk

Anche se siete stati vaccinati contro l'influenza, correte un piccolo rischio di ammalarvi.

Even if you've had a flu shot, you run a small risk of getting sick.

di nuovo in piedi

to be back on one's feet

Dopo due settimane a letto con la febbre, Franca è di nuovo in piedi.

After two weeks lying in bed with fever, Franca is back on her feet.

dare la carica

to give a boost, lit. to give a charge

Il caffè italiano ti dà la carica.

Italian coffee gives you a boost.

Death

avere un piede nella fossa

to have one foot in the grave

Teo ha un tumore al fegato. Ormai ha già un piede nella fossa.

Teo has a liver tumor. By now he's got one foot in the grave.

crepare

to die (used traditionally for animals and for humans in slang)

Che orrore, nessuno dovrebbe crepare in quel modo.

How awful, no one should die like that.

schiattare

to kick the bucket, lit. to collapse, to explode

I suoi genitori sono schiattati l'anno scorso in un incidente d'aereo.

His parents died last year in a plane crash.

R.I.P.

Did you know that for some time after death, your hair and nails continue to grow? It's not bad enough to die; you have to worry about trimming your toenails to feel comfortable in the rarely worn dress up shoes they're burying you in. The expression *tirare le cuoia*, "to pull the leathers," must be associated with the rigidity of the body after death. Poetry-inspired expressions like *andare agli alberi pizzuti*, are used in Rome and in the *Centro* where graves lie in the shade of cypress trees. *Arrivare al capolinea*, "to arrive at the end of the line," is a phrase that compares life with a bus or metro ride. We get on at one stop, get off at another, meet new passengers, and encounter mechanical problems. Like a bus route, life has its end too. Even the longest trip has to stop *un giorno o l'altro*. We all hope the *capolinea*, "end of the line," is still far away, if only the driver could just slow down a bit!

vegetale, m

vegetable

Dopo il suo ictus, il mio amico è diventato un vegetale.

After his stroke, my friend became a vegetable.

far secco qualcuno

to mow someone down, lit. to make someone dry

Il camionista si è addormentato e ha fatto secco un motociclista.
The truck driver fell asleep and mowed down a motorcyclist.

secco, secca
dead, lit. dried
Se l'ambulanza non si sbriga, saranno secchi!
If the ambulance doesn't hurry, they'll be dead.

New Life

piogge, fpl
period, lit. rains
Lara mi ha detto che le piogge erano quasi finite. Evviva, stasera si fa sesso!
Lara told me her period was almost over. Hurray, tonight we'll have sex!

alzare la bandiera rossa
to be on the rag, lit. to raise the red flag
Anna ha alzato la bandiera rossa.
Anna is on the rag.

avere le proprie cose/regole
to have one's period, lit. to have one's own things/rules
Non contraddite Jessica quando ha le sue cose!
Don't contradict Jessica when she has her period!

Khmer rossi, mpl
period, lit. Khmers rouges (communist Cambodian soldiers led by Pol Pot)

Sono arrivati i Khmer rossi, è per questo che Sarah è così permalosa.

Her period came, that's why Sarah's so irritable.

aver un bimbo in pancia

to be pregnant, lit. to have a baby in the tummy

Fatima ha un bimbo in pancia.

Fatima is pregnant.

avere una pagnotta nel forno

to have a bun in the oven

Ma non lo sapevi? Mara ha ancora una pagnotta nel forno.

Didn't you know it? Mara has another bun in the oven.

liberarsi di un bambino

to have an abortion, lit. to free oneself from a child

Dopo averci pensato sopra per lunghe settimane, Priscilla ha deciso di liberarsi del bambino.

After having thought about it for weeks, Priscilla decided to have an abortion.

CHAPTER THIRTEEN

Guerra e pace:

Looking for Trouble and Keeping the Peace

Italians are peaceful, but they also have strong temperaments and mood swings. *Il sangue italiano* or *il sangue latino* runs in their veins. This blood tends to boil easily, making Italians *scatenarsi*, "blow up violently." Thankfully, they also tend to cool off quickly, and it's usually *amici come prima*. Romans were big conquerors— they once fought for their unity and managed to get the three provinces of Veneto, Lombardia, and Friuli back from the dying Austro-Hungarian Empire.

Before and/or during World War II, the Italian army fought in Libya, Ethiopia, Eritrea, Greece, Spain (during the Spanish Civil War), and the Balkans. Unprepared for the Greeks' strong resistance, *l'esercito* had to call in the Germans to defeat *Grecia*. The precious weeks wasted in this war are, according to some historians, the reason the Russian campaign started so late. This is why Italy is often blamed (or thanked!) for the slowdown and eventual defeat of the Nazis. They may not be the best conquerors, but Italians feel strongly about defending their own lands. So if you've had one too many *grappa*, best not to pick a fight with any *Pinco Pallino*, Tom, Dick, or Harry.

Annoying

rompere/scassare le palle a qualcuno
to break someone's balls
Roberto ci rompe le palle con i suoi lamenti continui.
Roberto is breaking our balls with his continuous complaints.

dito nel culo, m
pain in the ass, unbearable, lit. finger in the ass
Isabella a volte è un dito nel culo.
Isabella is sometimes a pain in the ass.

DITO NEL CULO AND OTHER PAINS IN THE ASS

You'll hear many ways of saying *rompere le palle.* In some places, natives prefer *scassare* to *rompere.* Based on this expression you find *rompere le balle*, with the same vulgarity and meaning, *rompere i coglioni*, more vulgar, and *rompere le scatole*, less vulgar, (*scatole* meaning "boxes"). *Rompere* is also heard, as in *mi stai rompendo*, "you're annoying me." If you feel someone is draining you, then this person is the kind that *secca qualcuno*, "dries someone." You'll also hear *scocciare* in place of *seccare.* Pains in the ass are called *rompicoglioni, scassacoglioni, rompipalle, scassapalle, rompiscattole, seccatore, dito nel culo,* and *scocciatore.* Annoying animals and parasites have inspired other slang words as well. Like "pubic lice," *le piattole*, everyone wants to get laid, but nobody wants them, or *le sanguisuge*, "leeches." You may find plenty of *rompicoglioni* during your trip to Italy, so be prepared to tune out.

attaccabottoni, m, f
pain in the ass, lit. one who stitches to buttons

Tuo fratello è un attaccabottoni: ha parlato per ore e non mi voleva lasciare in pace.

Your brother is a pain in the ass: he spoke for hours and wouldn't leave me alone.

attaccare lite

to look for problems, lit. to attach a quarrel

Non attaccare lite con Pedro; se si arrabbia, ti distrugge.

Don't look for problems with Pedro; if he gets upset, he'll destroy you.

essere attaccato come un'ostrica a qualcuno/essere come una cozza sullo scoglio

to suffocate someone (in a relationship), lit. to be stuck like an oyster/to be like a mussel on the rock

Sei come una cozza sullo scoglio con il tuo ragazzo. Lascialo respirare!

Don't suffocate your boyfriend like glue. Let him breathe!

stare appiccato come un francobollo

to stick to someone like glue, lit. to be stuck like a stamp

Non starmi appiccicato come un francobollo, vai a bere qualcosa!

Don't stick to me like glue, go have a drink!

aggrapparsi ai coglioni di qualcuno

to be clingy, lit. to cling to someone's balls

Quando usciamo, Elio si aggrappa sempre ai miei coglioni. Non lo sopporto più.

When we go out, Elio's always too clingy. I can't stand him anymore.

fare cagare qualcuno

to annoy someone, lit. to make someone shit

Le tue lamentele mi fanno proprio cagare.

Your complaints are really annoying me.

giocare con il fuoco

to play with fire

Non dire che la mia ragazza è cretina. Stai giocando con il fuoco . . .

Don't call my girlfriend an idiot. You're playing with fire . . .

non dare tregua a qualcuno

to not give someone a break

Mio fratellino non dà tregua a mia madre; piange sempre.

My little brother doesn't give my mother a break; he's always crying.

stare addosso a qualcuno/non mollare qualcuno

to be all over/on someone's back, lit. to not let someone go

La mia prof di matematica mi sta sempre addosso.

My math teacher is always on my back.

seguire qualcuno come un cagnolino

to follow someone around like a puppy

Ovunque io vada mi segue come un cagnolino.

Everywhere I go, he follows me around like a puppy.

cercare rogne

to look/ask for trouble

Giorgio ha cercato rogne a Ted per tutto il giorno.

Giorgio has been asking for trouble with Ted all day long.

stancare qualcuno/le orecchie a qualcuno

to bore someone, lit. to tire someone/someone's ears

Non voglio più sentirti, Federico; mi stanchi di brutto!
I don't want to listen to you anymore, Federico; you really bore me.

gettare legna sul fuoco

to add fuel to the fire, lit. to throw wood on the fire
Ogni volta che Paolo diceva qualcosa, buttava legna sul fuoco.
Every time Paolo said something, he added fuel to the fire.

palloso, pallosa

annoying; from *palle*, balls
Me ne vado prima che arrivino mia sorella e la sua amica pallosa.
I'm leaving before my sister and her annoying friend arrive.

Beat it

ammazzarsi

to get lost, lit. to kill oneself
Ammazzati o Tibaldo ti fa a pezzi.
Get lost or Tibaldo will destroy you.

crepa stronzo, stronza!

eat shit and die!, lit. die, piece of shit!
Crepa stronzo! Se ti ritrovo per strada, ti spacco la faccia.
Eat shit and die! If I find you in my way again, I'll break your face.

andare fuori dalle palle

to beat it, lit. to go out of the balls
Andate tutti quanti fuori dalle palle. Ho detto che non volevo vedere nessuno.
All of you beat it. I said I didn't want to see anybody.

117

Italians also politely say andare fuori dalle scatole, *literally "to go out of the boxes." Andare* fuori dai piedi, levarsi dai piedi, *and* togliersi dai piedi *mean that someone is literally "stepping on your feet." You'll hear synonyms of* palle *in those genuine expressions:* andare fuori dalle balle *and* fuori dai coglioni. *The meaning stays the same but the expression with* coglione *is more vulgar.* Togliersi di mezzo, *literally "to put oneself away from the middle," is also directed to people in the way. Siciliani will send people to bed, saying* Va curcati! *And if only you could use your magic wand to make these people* sparire, *"disappear."*

stare zitto, zitta
shut up, lit. stay silent
Stai zitto, hai già combinato abbastanza casino.
Shut up, you already made enough mess.

lasciare stare qualcuno
to let someone be, lit. to let someone stay
Raga', lasciate stare Claudio. Ha avuto una giornataccia in ufficio.
Guys, let Claudio be. He had a terrible day at the office.

lasciare stare qualcosa
to let something go, lit. to let something stay
Il passato è passato. Lasciamo stare queste vecchie storie di famiglia.
Past is past. Let's let these old family stories go.

viaggiare
to back off, lit. to travel

Viaggia! Non m'interessi per niente.
Back off! I'm not interested in you at all.

chiudere il becco
to shut up, lit. to close the beak
Chiudi il becco, Caterina! Non tocca a te parlare!
Shut up, Caterina! It's not your turn to speak!

battibecco, m
argument, discussion, lit. that beats the beaks
Volete piantarla adesso con questi battibecchi?
You want to stop it with these arguments now?

farsi i cazzi/cavoli propri
to mind one's own business, lit. to make one's dicks/cabbages
Ma perché Luigia non si fa mai i cazzi suoi?
Why doesn't Luigia ever mind her own business?

piantarla/farla finita
to stop it, lit. to plant it/end it
Fatela finita! Sappiamo tutti che ci state mentendo.
Stop it! We all know you're lying to us.

In a Fight

fare/prendere a pugni qualcuno
to punch someone, lit. to make/take punches with someone
Davide e Mario hanno ancora fatto a pugni per una ragazza.
Once again, Davide and Mario punched each other over a girl.

prendere qualcuno a calci (nel culo)
to kick someone's ass, lit. to take someone with kicks (in the ass)

I genitori di Alessia l'hanno presa a calci nel culo quando è tornata a casa alle tre.

Alessia's parents kicked her ass when she came back home at 3 a.m.

prendere qualcuno a schiaffi

to slap someone, lit. to take someone with slaps

Quanto vorrei prendere a schiaffi il professore quando mi parla in quel modo!

How I'd like to slap my teacher when he speaks to me like that!

gonfiare di botte qualcuno

to beat the shit out of someone, lit. to inflate someone with whacks

Degli adolescenti hanno gonfiato di botte un barbone senza nessun motivo.

Teenagers kicked the shit out of a bum without a single reason.

dare una sberla

to slap, lit. to give a slap

Se mi dai ancora una sberla, telefono alla polizia.

If you slap me again, I'll call the police.

stendere qualcuno

to knock someone down, lit. to lay someone

Filippo ha steso Harry con un destro bene assestato.

Filippo knocked Harry down with a well-placed right.

cazzotto, m

punch; from *cazzo*, dick

Gianni non ha potuto evitare il cazzotto di Giacomo.

Gianni was unable to avoid Giacomo's punch.

fare a pezzi qualcuno

to beat the shit out of someone, lit. to do someone to pieces

Una banda di minorenni ha fatto a pezzi il figlio della mia vicina.
A teenage gang beat the shit out of my neighbor's son.

pestare
to kick
I bambini hanno pestato il prete perché aveva molestato uno di loro.
The children kicked the priest because he had abused one of them.

fregarsene
to not give a shit; from *frega*, pussy
Sua moglie gli fa le corna e Carlo se ne frega. Che strana coppia!
His wife is cheating on him and Carlo doesn't give a shit. What a strange couple!

farsi un baffo di qualcosa
to care less, lit. to grow a moustache of something
Mi faccio un baffo se sei contenta o meno.
I could care less if you're happy or not.
Lit. I grow a moustache if you're happy or less.

infischiarsene di qualcosa/qualcuni
to not give a damn; from *fischiare*, to whistle
Bobby se ne infischia di tutto e tutti.
Bobby doesn't give a damn about anyone or anything.

sorbirsi qualcuno
to put up with someone, lit. to drink someone
Ci siamo dovuti sorbire il suo fratellino invece di uscire ed spassarcela.
We had to put up with her little brother instead of going out and having fun.

CHAPTER FOURTEEN

Che follia!:

Life is a Cabaret ... or Stadium ... or Discotheque

Italians love going out in groups. Even before kids learn to drive a Vespa or party at the local discotheque, they've already made their way *sul muretto*. Later, while going to a pub, disco, or movie theater, young Italians form a close clan. If ancient Romans asked only for bread and games at the *Colosseo*, nowadays Italians could be happy with sex, pizza, *calcio*, and of course discos. Sex is apparent in all places: most Italian TV shows feature sexy scantily-clad women . . . imagine *The Price is Right* with bikini-clad supermodels. The "high ratings," *l'alto tasso d'ascolto*, prove Italians love it. Sexily dressed women make a stupid show watchable.

It's also no surprise then that, despite the beauty of the Italian Alps, Italians prefer to spend their *agosto* holiday *al mare* surrounded by wonderful topless creatures. Cities like *Rimini* and nearby *Riccione* on the Adriatic coast are a must for teenagers. While the day is dedicated to the beach, the night is all about a wild party. The amazing number of pubs and discos has made these cities the highlight of *il divertimento all'italiana*, entertainment "Italian style."

Enjoying

scatenarsi

to let loose, lit. to unleash oneself

Ogni sabato sera, Andrea si scatena in discoteca.

Every Saturday night, Andrea lets loose at the disco.

divertirsi un pacco/mondo/casino

to amuse oneself a lot, lit. to amuse oneself a pack/world/brothel

Elisa e Patrizia si divertono un mondo a sparlare di te.

Elisa and Patrizia amuse themselves a lot by bitching about you.

darsi alla pazza gioia

to have fun, lit. to give oneself to insane joy

I figli di Brenda si davano alla pazza gioia mentre puliva la casa.

Brenda's children were out having fun while she was cleaning the house.

chiuso, chiusa come un riccio

shy as a mouse, lit. as closed as a hedgehog

Da quando è arrivato in classe, il nuovo allievo è rimasto chiuso come un riccio.

Since he entered the classroom, the new student has been shy as a mouse.

spassarsela (Nord)

to have fun; from the German *Spass*, fun

Quando Alessandra non lavora, pensa solo a spassarsela.

When Alessandra doesn't work, she just thinks of having fun.

Staying Home

pantofolaio, pantofolaia
homebody; from *pantofola*, slipper
Aida non sopporta i pantofolai.
Aida can't stand homebodies.

andare a nanna
to go to bed; from *nanna*, childish term for sleep
Mi spiace, non uscirò con voi ragazzi. Devo andare a nanna.
Sorry, I'm not going out with you guys. I have to go to bed.

fare un pisolino
to take a nap
Enrico non ti può rispondere adesso; sta facendo un pisolino.
Enrico can't answer you now; he's taking a nap.

sogni d'oro
sweet dreams, lit. golden dreams
Sogni d'oro amore mio!
Sweet dreams my love!

tv spazzatura, f
reality show, lit. garbage TV
Cecilia va pazza per la tv spazzatura.
Cecilia is crazy about reality shows.

tivù, f
TV; from "T" and "V," *ti* and *vu*
Simone preferisce guardare la tivù invece di portar fuori il cane.
Simone prefers to watch TV rather than take the dog out.

scannatoio, m

bachelor pad/slaughterhouse

Luca ha comprato un monolocale in città che gli serve da scannatoio.

Luca bought a one bedroom flat in the city that he uses as a bachelor pad.

Going Out

andare in giro

to wander/go out, lit. to go on tour

Andate in giro stasera?

Are you going out tonight?

andare a zonzo

to wander around

Siamo andati a zonzo per ore a Venezia.

We spent hours wandering around Venice.

passare la notte in bianco

to pull an all-nighter, lit. to pass the night in white

Mia sorella ha passato ancora la notte in bianco coi suoi amici.

My sister pulled an all-nighter again with her friends.

locale, m

pub, night club, lit. room

Marco ha aperto un locale alla periferia di Milano. Tutti i weekend ha circa duecento clienti.

Marco opened a pub in the suburbs of Milan. Every weekend he has about two hundred customers.

fare le ore piccole

to stay out until the wee hours, lit. to make the small hours

E' mio compleanno e prevedo di fare le ore piccole.

It's my birthday and I'm counting on staying out until the wee hours.

fare una levataccia

to get up early; from *levare*, to take off and the suffix *-accia*

Per evitare il traffico in autostrada, dovremmo fare una levataccia.

In order to avoid traffic on the freeway, we'll have to get up early.

andare a vedere la partita

to go see a match (soccer)

Tutti gli uomini della famiglia sono andati a vedere la partita allo stadio.

All the men in the family went to see the match at the stadium.

azzurri, mpl

Italian national soccer team, lit. the sky-blue ones

Senza sorpresa, gli azzurri hanno vinto il mondiale.

Not surprisingly, the Italian soccer team won the world championship.

evviva

hurray, long live; from *e* and *viva*, the subjunctive of *vivere*, to live

Evviva l'Italia! Siamo i migliori!

Long live Italy! We're the best!

tifoso, tifosa

fan

I tifosi della Lazio e del Milan hanno fatto a pugni dopo la partita.

Fans of Lazio and Milan fought each other after the match.

tifare/fare il tifo per qualcuno

to root for someone, lit. to make the fan for someone

Alessandro è Milanese, ma non tifa né per l'Inter né per il Milan.

Alessandro is Milanese, but he roots for neither Inter nor Milan.

teppista, m

hooligan, lit. delinquent

I teppisti si sono scontrati con i poliziotti.

The hooligans locked horns with the policemen.

A HISTORY OF VIOLENCE:

Italians love *il calcio* as much as they love *i Gran Premi*. They're passionate and very proud of their sports teams, cars, motorcycles, and pilots. National pride may be understandable in international competition, but what happens in the national soccer championship takes the cake. Fan clubs revert to Neanderthal behavior, with no respect for other fans or their property. Certain groups are even openly neofascist. The year 2007 was a bad one for Italian soccer. *Tifosi, teppisti*, and policemen fought each other on many occasions. In spring 2007, *un ispettore dei carabinieri* was killed by a group of *tifosi catanesi*. Nine months later, *un tifoso laziale* was shot by a policeman on the hood of a car and even if it had nothing to do with soccer, riots followed in his *città*. Score, one to one . . . Twice that same year, the Italian championship was stopped, and later only stadiums with good security were allowed to let fans in. Everywhere else, games were played *a porte chiuse*, "with closed doors."

andare al cinema

to go to the movies, lit. to go to the movie theater

Che facciamo? Vi va di andare al cinema?

What are we doing? Would you like to go to the movies?

farsi una birra

to go have a beer, lit. to make oneself a beer

Che noia stare a casa; facciamoci una birra!

What a bore to stay home; let's go have a beer!

farsi una pizza

to go have a pizza, lit. to make oneself a pizza

Matteo e Paolo sono andati a farsi una pizza.

Matteo and Paolo went to have a pizza.

Parties and Discos

rimbalzare qualcuno (Nord)

to refuse entry/reject, lit. to rebound, to bounce back

Mi hanno rimbalzato all'entrata del club.

They rejected me at the night club entrance.

guastafeste, m, f

party pooper, lit. party spoiler

La tua festa sarebbe stata perfetta se non fosse per quel guastafeste di tuo fratello.

Your party would have been perfect if it hadn't been for your brother the party pooper.

macello, m

mess, lit. butchery

Dopo aver dato un party, la casa era un vero macello.

After I had a party, the house was a real mess.

casino, m

mess/racket, lit. brothel

I vicini di casa hanno fatto un casino incredibile ieri sera.
The neighbors made an unbelievable racket last night.

fare baldoria
to revel/paint the town red, lit. to make festivities
Gli invitati hanno fatto baldoria.
The guests painted the town red.

ragazza immagine, f
hostess/attractive woman paid to entertain clients at bars, drawing in a crowd, lit. image girl
Le ragazze immagine di questo locale sono delle vere bombe.
This pub's hostesses are real hotties.

buttarsi in pista
to throw oneself on the dance floor
La mia ragazza si è buttata in pista appena entrata nel locale.
My girlfriend threw herself on the dance floor as soon as she entered the club.

avere il ritmo nel sangue
to have rhythm in one's blood
Barbara ha il ritmo nel sangue. Guarda come si muove . . .
Barbara has rhythm in her blood. Look how she moves . . .

buttafuori/buttadentro, m
bouncer, lit. who throws outside/inside
Il buttafuori non ha lasciato entrare Jack in discoteca.
The bouncer didn't let Jack enter the discotheque.

ragazzo, ragazza cubo/cubisto, cubista
go-go dancer, lit. cube boy, girl/cubist

Arturo ci ha provato con tutte le cubiste del night.
Arturo tried with every go-go dancer in the club.

mondo della notte, m
nightlife
Astrid ama così tanto il mondo della notte che vuole
lavorare in un night.
Astrid loves the nightlife so much that she wants to work in a club.

Leaving

alzare le chiappe
to bust a move, lit. to lift up the butt cheeks
Alziamo le chiappe, ragazzi. Mi sono seccato.
Let's bust a move, guys. I'm bored.

scrostarsi
to move/get off, lit. to remove oneself; from *crosta*, crust
"Bambini, scrostatevi dal mio divano!" disse il padre.
"Kids, get off my couch!" said the father.

CHAPTER FIFTEEN

Piaceri proibiti:

Forbidden Pleasures

When life provides you with all you need, you get bored. Breaking the law appears as a new side to explore. The dark side of Italian culture is found in the seedy districts of town at sundown. The two main problems Italy faces are drugs and prostitution, and the country counts more than 50,000 prostitutes and sex slaves. These include minors, but the vast majority is African followed by Eastern European, many whose home countries have recently joined the European Union. Prostitution is a 90,000,000 euro per month business. A full 40 percent of the action takes place in *Milano* and 20 percent in *Torino*, the cities with the highest per capita income.

Some cities have changed their zoning systems to allow prostitution only in certain quarters, while others have forbidden driving at night or have declared prostitution illegal. *La legge Merlin*, Merlin's Law, aimed to eradicate *lo sfruttameno delle prostitute* by closing the brothels. As a result, pimps just made their women work the streets.

Any decision made just moves the problem from one block to the other or from one city to another, never to be fully resolved.

Successive governments have come to the same conclusion: it's hard to make an Italian adopt a more civil way of behaving.

Today the situation continues to worsen. To take back their streets, some Christian lobbies are trying to get a law passed that will punish the customers too—a first in Italy.

Drugs

deca di fumo, m
dose of shit, lit. ten (10,000 lire) of smoke
Tamara ha comprato due deca di fumo.
Tamara bought two doses of shit.

spinello, m/sigaretta mista, f
(mixed with tobacco) joint
Jonathan si è fumato uno spinello nel cortile della scuola.
Jonathan smoked a joint in the school courtyard.

purino, m
joint, lit. little pure one
Da quando ha saputo dei rischi dovuti al tabacco, Alfio fuma solo purini.
Since he heard about the dangers of tobacco, Alfio smokes only joints.

farsi una canna
to smoke a joint, lit. to make oneself a cane
Fatti una canna, rilassati.
Smoke a joint, relax.

erba, f
weed

Qualcuno fuma erba qui vicino.
Someone's smoking weed nearby.

Basilico *and* origano *are not only to be found on pizza or Italian pasta. Their strong smell and appearance led to their use as slang terms for marijuana. If you're ready to smoke, just say* fumo *or* mufo, *or ask for some ganja, cannabis, or marijuana. Some Italians may refer to hashish by giving its production zone or nationality of the dealer: you'll hear* l'albanaccio, *literally "the bad Albanian," and* l'afgano, *"the Afghan."*

ammazzare
to kill (alcohol or joint)
Non fare girare lo spinello; ammazzalo pure.
Don't pass the joint anymore; kill it.

tiro, m
drag, lit. shoot
Dammi un tiro, fratello!
Give me a drag, bro!

farsi un ping-pong
to share a joint, lit. to play ping-pong
Che noia; usciamo a farci un ping-pong.
What a bore; let's go out and share a joint.

pagliare/gremare
to smoke; from *paglia*, straw, to burn
Non si può più pagliare nei bar.
We can't smoke in pubs anymore.

133

paglia/bionda, f

ciggy, lit. straw/blond one

Dammi una paglia!

Give me a ciggy!

spacciatore, spacciatrice/spaccino, spaccina

dealer; lit. from *spacciare*, to sell

La pola arresta gli spacciatori ma i pezzi grossi non li prende mai.

Cops arrest petty drug dealers but they never catch the big shots.

bucarsi/farsi una pera

to shoot up, lit. to make holes in oneself/to make oneself a pear

Dei drogati si bucano dinanzi a casa mia.

Some drug addicts shoot up in front of my house.

bucato, bucata

junkie, lit. with holes

La stazione era il punto di raduno di bucati e spacciatori.

The railway station was the meeting point of junkies and drug dealers.

tossico, tossica

addict, abbr. of *tossicodipendente*

I tossici hanno invaso i giardini pubblici e nessuno ci si avventura di notte.

Addicts have invaded public gardens and no one dares to enter them at night.

bucomane, m, f

junkie, addict, concatenation of *buco*, hole, and *tossicomane*, drug addict

Dopo essere stato licenziato, Flavio è diventato un bucomane.

After he got fired, Flavio became a junkie.

spada, f

syringe, lit. swear

Non toccare questa spada! Se ti pungi puoi beccarti l'AIDS.

Don't touch that syringe! If you hurt yourself, you could get AIDS.

ero, f

heroine, smack, abbr. of *eroina*

Moreno è morto per un overdose d'ero.

Moreno died from an overdose of smack.

aristocratica, f

cocaine, blow, lit. aristocratic one

L'aristocratica si è popolarizzata.

Blow has become very popular.

Cocaine, once reserved for the higher classes, is now present in even the smallest villages. Its color inspired slang such as bianca, neve, or fioca, "snow." White dust on a coffee table can be something other than cocaine; don't jump to conclusions! It may just be un po' di polvere, "a little bit of dust," talco, "talcum powder," zucchero, "sugar," or some traces of bug repellent, nafta, "naphthalene."

sniffare

to sniff

I bambini delle strade sniffano colla.

Street children sniff glue.

farsi una cannuccia, f

to sniff cocaine, lit. to make oneself a straw

Come faccio a farmi una cannuccia adesso che mi hai spaccato il naso?

How am I going to sniff cocaine now that you've broken my nose?

sciare

to do lines of coke, lit. to ski

Non serve andare in montagna per sciare . . .

You don't need to go to the mountains to do lines of coke...

Lit. You don't need to go to the mountains to ski...

andato, andata

gone (high)

Mario è andato del tutto. Non fare caso a quello che dice.

Mario's gone. Don't pay attention to what he says.

farsi un trip/acido

to trip/drop acid, lit. to make oneself a trip/an acid

In discoteca, Sofia si è fatta un acido per la prima volta.

At the discotheque, Sofia dropped acid for the first time.

impasticcato, impasticcata

high; from *pasticca*, pill

Era ovvio che Chiara era impasticcata.

It was obvious Chiara was high.

Prostitution

troia, f
slut, lit. sow
Laudia è una troia. Se la fa con chiunque.
Laudia is a slut. She does it with everyone.

puttana, f
whore
Silvia fa la puttana.
Silvia is a whore.

PUTTANA!

It's not good to be *una puttana* in Italy. While the Old Testament says prostitution is a sin, the New Testament condemns it, but forgives it too. It seems that religious Italians read only the first part of the Bible. *Svergognata*, "ashamed woman," is used by older generations and confirms this. When speaking of prostitutes, Italians tend to use depictive words. Her lighthearted ways make her look like a "quail," *una quaglia*. She is also compared to a *lucciola*, "firefly," because of the fires the hookers make to keep warm in the streets. As all entomologists know, only the female firefly makes light at night to attract the male and let them know her exact location. Johns are attracted to the lights, and if the lady's intention wasn't sexual, the result is the same. The sound of her *tacchi a spillo*, "high heels," hitting the *marciapede* inspired *battona*, *battistrada*, "one who beats (the road)," and *zoccola* from the wooden shoes prostitutes wore in the olden days. Their constant *viavai* led them to be called *passeggiatrici*, "streetwalkers." Regional slang is also popular: *baldracca* and *sgualdrina* are common in the north. The Roman term *mignotta*, may come from the French *mignonne*, "cutie," but here's another hypothesis: *mignotta* may come from two words put on abandoned children's identity bracelets: *mater ignotae*, "unknown mother," m *ignotae*. If this is the case, Italian may be the only language to call a prostitute after her child's civil or social status.

puttaneggiare
to act like a whore
Se la mia ragazza puttaneggia con un altro tipo, la mollo.
If my girlfriend acts like a whore with another guy, I'll leave her.

puttanesco, puttanesca
whorish, slutty, lit. like a whore
Giovanni ama le ragazze che portano vestiti puttaneschi.
Giovanni likes girls who wear slutty clothes.

puttaniere, m
whoremonger, John, lit. who uses the services of prostitutes
Non farti passare per un santo. Sappiamo tutti che sei un lurido puttaniere.
Don't pretend you're a saint. We all know you're a filthy John.

bordello/locale a luci rosse, m
brothel; from the French *bordel*, red light club
Le autorità hanno chiuso tutti i bordelli, ma lasciano aprire i saloni di massaggi.
The authorities closed all the brothels, but they let people open massage parlors.

Le case di piacere *were legalized in the middle of the 19th century to satisfy the needs of French soldiers who helped Italians fight the Austrians for their freedom. By law they had to keep the blinds closed, which gave birth to the term* casa chiusa. Casino *and* bordello *were once used only for brothels, but now they're synonymous with a big mess or racket. What better word than* puttanaio *to inform people of what is inside it:* puttane*? Based on the same principle,* l'uccellatoio *is the place where birds (dicks) hide.*

(ragazza) squillo, f

escort girl, lit. phone ring (girl)

Per non uscire da solo, Kevin ha chiamato una squillo, ma lei gli ha dato buca.

In order not to go out alone, Kevin called an escort girl, but she didn't show.

magnaccia/pappone, m

pimp; from Romano *magnare*, to eat/big eater (pimps "eat" the money)

Gli sbirri cercano il magnaccia della puttana ammazzata.

The cops are looking for the dead hooker's pimp.

Madama, f

Madam

Pochi sanno chi sia la Madama di questo bordello.

Only few people know who the Madam of this brothel is.

CHAPTER SIXTEEN

La bella e la bestia:
She/He's Got the Look

Italy is a land of beauty and fashion. Splendid actresses like Sofia Loren and the voluptuous Gina Lolobrigida made voluptuous beauty famous the world over. *Le passerelle di Milano e di Roma*, "Milan and Rome's catwalks," helped Italian designers rise to the top. Many brands of clothing as well as renowned couturiers have Italian origins. Armani, Versace, and Valentino are brands that everybody knows. In his field, Benetton has had the same impact. Looks in general are very important to Italians. Whether in cities or the countryside, different fashions are shared by communities, groups, or friends.

The cliché of the macho Italian man is no longer true in some respects. Italian men look more and more *metrosessuali* and foreigners have difficulties distinguishing a straight Italian from a gay one. Never underestimate how vital fashion is to every *strato* of society: *nelle gallerie Vittorio Emmanuele*, Milan's celebrated indoor "mall," even *i carabinieri* wear designer uniforms offered by the luxury shop tenants in order to keep a very high fashion standard in the area.

Beauty Contest

pezzo di figa/pezzo di gnocca
hottie, lit. piece of pussy
Penelope è un bel pezzo di figa. A tutti piacerebbe uscire con lei.
Penelope is a hottie. Everyone would like to go out with her.

figo, figa
handsome, pretty, sexy; from *figa*, pussy
Sei troppo figa quando ti metti un costume da bagno.
You're so sexy when you put on a bathing suit.

gnocco, gnocca (also adjective)
hottie, sexy, lit. potato dumpling, also pussy
Le ragazze con le quali Leandro è uscito erano tutte gnocche, ma quanto erano stupide!
The girls Leandro dated were all hotties, but how stupid they were!

Beauty surrounds you here in Italy, but your politically correct American upbringing may make you afraid to use the words above. No matter, here is some less hip but also less sexist slang: il chicco, *seed, and* la chicca, *"sweet," are often used for sweetie or doll, but* una ragazzina *can also be una chicca, "a beauty." Italians are obsessed with food;* un bel bocconcino, *literally "a nice mouthful," and* bona *(from* buona, *"good") target hotties.*

ciospo, m

dog (unattractive person); concatenation of *cesso* and *rospo*, toilet and toad

Come può uscire con Valentina? Non lo vede che è un ciospo?

How can he go out with Valentina? Can't he see she's a dog?

cozza, f

dog (ugly woman), lit. mussel

Stasera si va a caccia di cozze!

Tonight we go dog hunting!

antistupro, m

something or someone ugly, unflattering. lit. against rape

Non mettere quel maglione, è un antistupro.

Don't wear that sweater, it's really unflattering.

Silhouette

carrozzeria, f

sexual attributes of a woman, silhouette, lit. car body

Nicoletta aveva una bella carrozzeria prima di sposarsi . . .

Nicoletta had a nice silhouette before getting married . . .

curve, fpl

curves

Jessica ha delle curve da sogno.

Jessica has dream curves.

tette, fpl

tits; from *tettare*, to teat

Secondo me, quelle sono tette finte.
I'd say they're fake tits.

TITTIES, A MATTER OF SIZE:

I seni, the breasts, are more often called *le tette, le zinne (Centro), le poppe*, or *le ciocce*. Other, more visual, expressions insist on size and shape, *i meloni*, "melons," and *gli airbags*. In the same vein, men will admire *i polmoni*, a woman's "lungs." Usually a chick with big tits is called *una tettona, una latteria*, or *una fabbrica di latte*, "a milk factory." On the opposite end of the spectrum, a flat-chested or bony woman is called *un'autostrada*, "a freeway," or *un asse da stiro*, "an ironing board."

culetto, m
small ass
Ma guarda un po' che bei culetti!
Look at those small asses!

canestro, m
butt, lit. basket
Sergio va nei luoghi affollati per toccare i canestri delle signore. Che porco!
Sergio goes to crowded places to touch women's butts. What a pig!

The shape of the ass can be reminiscent of un man-dolino, un contrabbasso, *or* un tamburo, *"a drum." A huge round bottle of about 52 liters,* la damigiana, *from* dama Giana, *"Madame Giana," refers to big asses, while* il fondoschiena, *"the bottom of the back," and* il didietro, *"the behind," are more respectful. When*

Italians are pulling someone's leg, they say Ti prendo per i fondelli, *or* Ti stoprendendo per il culo, *literally "I'm taking you in the ass," best translated into English as, "I'm just f**king with you." A girl with junk in the trunk is called* una culona, *while* culo, culatone, *and* culone *refer to men who use their ass with the same sex.*

chiappona, f
woman with a big ass, lit. who has big *chiappe*, ass cheeks
Non so perché Pippo preferisce le chiappone.
I don't know why Pippo prefers chicks with big asses.

On the Body

lana, f
thick hair, lit. wool
In autunno il mio cane perde tanta lana.
In autumn my dog loses a lot of hair.

pelata, pelato
bald, lit. peeled
Paulo è mezzo cieco e quasi tutto pelato.
Paulo is half-blind and almost completely bald.

zucca/cocuzza, f/cocomero, m
gourd
Ma non ha proprio niente in zucca!
She does have really nothing in her gourd!

orecchie a sventola, fpl
Dumbo ears, lit. slap ears

Anche sua madre ha le orecchie a sventola!
His mother has Dumbo ears too!

fari, mpl

eyes, lit. car lights
Hai visto che fari azzurri aveva quel tipo?
Did you see what wonderful blue eyes that guy had?

muso, m

nose, lit. muzzle
Mi sono spaccato il muso cadendo per terra.
I broke my nose falling on the floor.

naso alla francese, m

ski jump nose, lit. French nose
Pippo ha un naso alla francese.
Pippo has a ski jump nose.

becco, m

mouth, lit. beak
Chiudi il becco quando parlo.
Shut up when I'm talking.
Lit. Close your beak when I'm talking.

zanna, f (Nord)

tooth; from the German *Zahn*, tooth
Costantino non sorride mai sulle foto perché gli mancano due zanne di davanti.
Costantino never smiles in pictures because he's missing two front teeth.

zampa, f

arm/leg/hand, lit. paw

Silvio si è spaccato la zampa sciando.
Silvio broke his leg skiing.

tappo, m
stump, lit. cork
Beatrice è alta e magra, ma suo fratello è un tappo.
Beatrice is tall and thin, but her brother is a stump.

lampione, m
string bean, lit. streetlight
I figli di Linda sono tutti lampioni.
Linda's sons are all string beans.

ciccia, f
fat, weight
**La sua ragazza vuole perdere un po' di ciccia prima di
andare in vacanza al mare.**
*His girlfriend wants to lose some weight before going on vacation
to the sea.*

cicciolina/ciccia, f
sweetie, lit. little fat one
Ciccia, vieni un attimo qua.
Sweetie, come here for awhile.

GREASE AND FAT:

A lot of pasta topped with delicious sauces, combined with no
exercise, can wreak havoc on your figure. In a country ruled by
appearance, Italians are not especially kind to overweight people. *Ciccia* gave way to *cicciona*, "fat woman" and *cicciabomba*,
literally "fat bomb." *Babbiona* is not nice either; it's applied to
fat, ugly, or stupid old women. You'll also hear *ciccia*, "fat," and

cicciolina, "little fat one," as sweet talk between couples. Be careful though—these terms of endearment must be used carefully. *Cicciolina* was also the name of *una pornodiva*, imported from Hungary by an Italian who invented her stage name to glorify her curves. Even more surprising, Ilona Staller was the first ex-porn star in the world to be elected to Parliament. In 1987 her party, *il partito dell'amore*, "the Love Party,"won a seat *alla Camera dei Deputati*, the Italian equivalent of Congress.

allettante
sexy; lit. from *latte*, milk
Il suo fisico allettante ne fa sognare più d'uno.
Her sexy body makes more than one man dream of her.

Clothes and Accessories

basco, m
hat, lit. bask
Felice cerca dappertutto il basco.
Felice is looking everywhere for his hat.

quattr'occhi, mpl
four eyes
Quattr'occhi stai zitto!
Shut up four eyes!

reggitette/reggipoppe, m
bra, lit. boob holder
In Europa è difficile trovare reggitette grandi come i tuoi.
In Europe it's difficult to find big bras like yours.

essere di un'altra (Bologna)

to be beyond comparison, lit. to be from another (category, quality)

Ho comprato un bel vestito che è di un'altra!

I bought a nice suit that is beyond comparison!

stare da Dio/a pennello

to suit perfectly, to stay like God/ the paintbrush way

Questo tailleur ti sta a pennello, Jenna; dovresti comprarlo.

This suit fits you perfectly, Jenna; you should buy it.

farsi bello

to doll oneself up, lit. to make oneself cute

Cristina si è fatta bella per stasera. C'era molto lavoro da fare.

Cristina dolled herself up for this evening. There was a lot of work to do.

conciarsi male

to dress badly, lit. to dirt oneself

Come vi siete conciati male per il battesimo di vostra figlia! Vergogna.

How you were badly dressed at your daughter's baptism! Shame on you.

Looking one's best is some kind of a national sport. Every occasion is good for showing off. You don't need to go to a party per vestirti a festa, "to wear party clothes." With shiny shoes and gel in your hair, you'll literally be tirato a lucido, "pulled to the shine," or messo in tiro. In your expensive designer suit, visiting Italy's chicest

cities, you may hear guarda che pinguino, *"look, what a penguin."* No need to look around, or ask yourself if Italy's climate is not too hot for penguins. This time il pinguino *is the person you winked at in the mirror before you went out dressed to kill.*

minigonna giropassera, f

tiny miniskirt, lit. miniskirt that turns around the pussy
Selena va in giro con la minigonna giropassera.
Selena walks around with a tiny miniskirt.

vestiti firmati/griffati

designer clothes, lit. signed/scratched clothes
Non tutti si possono permettere vestiti griffati.
Not everyone can afford designer clothes.

nuovo di zecca/ pacca

brand new, lit. new from the money press/new from the package
Charlie esce ogni weekend con vestiti nuovi di pacca.
Charlie goes out every weekend wearing brand new clothes.

stracci, mpl

clothes, lit. rags
Adolfo ha comprato tanti stracci al mercatino dell'usato.
Adolfo bought a lot of clothes at the secondhand shop.

bottega, f

zipper, fly, lit. shop, boutique
Domenico ha sempre la bottega aperta.
Domenico's zipper is always open.

fanga, f (Bologna)

shoe; from *fango*, mud

Sara non sa dove ha messo le nuove fanghe.
Sara doesn't know where she put her new shoes.

trampoli, fpl
high heels, stilettos, lit. stilts
Fabrizia ha comprato un paio di trampoli.
Fabrizia bought a pair of high heels.

autoreggenti, fpl
thigh-highs, lit. self-supporting
Saresti molto più sexy con le autoreggenti!
You'd be much sexier with thigh-highs!

CHAPTER SEVENTEEN

ITALIAN
READER
ADVISORY

La bella e la bestia II:

Looks Aren't Everything

La botte can't be reduced to only fashion. During *il Rinascimento*, for example, other values such as intelligence and knowledge were celebrated. Ever heard of da Vinci or Michelangelo (not the Teenage Mutant Ninja Turtles)? It's easy to *giudicare una persona, "judge someone,"* by his or her physique or looks. In the olden days when fancy clothes, accessories, and perfume were inaccessible for most of the people, defining others by their character and way of being was a good traditional solution. *Coraggio*, sense of humor, humility, and *energia* are the common interpersonal *differenze* that people focus on. The lack of one or the excess of the other have inspired many interesting colloquial expressions.

Matusalemme/Matusa, m
old fart/fogey, lit. Methuselah
Mia figlia mi ha dato del Matusa perché non l'ho lasciata uscire con il suo ragazzo in settimana.
My daughter called me an old fogey because I wouldn't let her go out with her boyfriend during the week.

sapere ancora di latte

to be too young and inexperienced, lit. to still taste like (maternal) milk

Zitta! Sai ancora di latte. Questi sono discorsi da adulti.

Shut up! You're too young. These are adult discussions.

beghino, beghina

devout

Quelle vecchie vedove vanno in chiesa tutti i giorni; sono proprio delle beghine.

Those old widows go to church every day; they're really devout.

bigotta/santocchia/santarellina, f

hypocrite, lit. saint with the *-occhia/-ellina* suffixes

La vedo in chiesa ogni domenica, ma viene solo per farsi vedere. Che santocchia!

I see her in church every Sunday, but she comes just to show off. What a hypocrite!

fare la cornacchia

to gossip, lit. to play the crow

Smettila di fare la cornacchia. Non voglio sapere niente di tutto questo.

Stop gossiping. I don't want to hear anything of this.

cafone, cafona

boor

Flavio, non fare il cafone a casa di tua nonna!

Flavio, don't be such a boor at your grandmother's house!

leccaculo/leccapiedi, m, f

ass-kisser, lit. ass-licker/feet-licker

Non fare il leccaculo con me.

Don't play the ass-kisser with me.

ruffiano, ruffiana (Sicily)
bootlicker
Dovevi sentirla quando parlava con il direttore. Che ruffiana!
You should have heard her speaking to the director. What a bootlicker!

stronzo, stronza
bastard, lit. turd
Non fare lo stronzo, Tino, dammi cinque euro. Te li rendo appena posso.
Don't be a bastard, Tino, give me five euro. I'll give them back to you as soon as I can.

avere fegato/le palle/lo spessore
to have the guts/balls, lit. to have liver/the balls/the width
Dimmi in faccia ciò che racconti alle mie spalle se hai le palle.
Tell me to my face what you said behind my back if you've got the balls.

smidollato, smidollata/ pappamolle, m, f
coward, lit. spineless/soft babyfood
Vittorio ti ha rubato la ragazza e tu non reagisci? Che smidollato!
Vittorio took your girlfriend away from you and you don't say a word about it? What a coward!

nascere sotto una buona stella
to be born under a good star
Giancarlo è nato sotto una buona stella. Ha creato una ditta due anni fa che è ora leader mondiale nel suo campo.

Giancarlo has to be born under a good star. He founded a company two years ago that is the world leader in its field today.

avere culo

to be lucky, lit. to have ass

Basta, non gioco più con te. Hai troppo culo.

Enough, I won't play against you anymore. You're too lucky.

botta di culo, f

stroke of good luck, lit. hit of ass

Abbiamo trovato un posteggio a due passi del locale. Che botta di culo!

We found a parking space very close to the club. What a stroke of good luck!

essere infognato/inculato

to be extremely lucky, lit. to be sewed/f**ked in the ass

Mia zia è infognata. Vince sempre a briscola.

My aunt is extremely lucky. She wins every briscola game.

stare allo scherzo

to have a sense of humor, lit. to stay at the joke

Non c'è niente da fare. Il prof non sta affatto allo scherzo.

There's nothing to do. The teacher has no sense of humor at all.

raccontare balle/palle

to bullshit, lit. to tell balls

Ludovico ha raccontato tante balle che nessuno non lo crede più.

Ludovico bullshitted so much that nobody believes him now.

sparare cavolate/stronzate

to spew bullshit, lit. to shoot bullshit (stuffs made of cabbage/turd)

Perché spari sempre cavolate?
Why are you always spewing bullshit?

prendere in giro/per il culo qualcuno

to take someone for a ride/f**k with someone, lit. to take some-
one around/by the ass
Ragazzi, non prendetemi in giro. Devo sapere la verità.
Guys, don't take me for a ride. I need to know the truth.

fare fesso qualcuno

to pull someone's leg, lit. to make someone dumb
È facilissimo fare fessa Loredana.
It's easy to pull Loredana's leg.

menefreghista, m, f

one who doesn't care; from *me ne frego*, I don't give a shit
Certo che se siamo tutti menefreghista, niente cambierà.
It's certain that if we all don't care, nothing will change.

fregarsene

to not give a shit; from *frega*, pussy
Me ne frego se riferisci tutto a tua madre.
I don't give a shit if you report everything to your mother.

parassita, m

mooch, lit. parasite
**A trenta anni vive ancora a scrocco dei suoi. Che
parassita!**
*Thirty years old and he's still living off his parents. What a
mooch!*

essere come il prezzemolo

to be everywhere, lit. to be like parsley
A Milano, i terroni sono come il prezzemolo.
In Milan, southerners are everywhere.

chiuso, chiusa come un'ostrica

closed-minded, lit. as closed as a mussel

Ho provato più volte a fargli cambiare idea, ma Lucio è chiuso come un'ostrica.

I tried many times to make him change his mind, but Lucio is closed-minded.

mettere i puntini sulle "I"

to dot one's "Is" and cross one's "Ts"

Gianni deve sempre mettere i puntini sulle "I."

Gianni has to always dot his "Is" and cross his "Ts."

pignolo, pignola

scrupulous

Samara è una donna pignola, quasi rompicoglioni.

Samara is a scrupulous woman, almost a pain in the ass.

stufo, stufa

tired/bored

Antonio è stufo del suo lavoro. Si vuole godere una bella vacanza.

Antonio is bored with his work. He wants to take a nice vacation.

ficcanaso, m, f

nosy, lit. who puts the nose inside

Dino è un ficcanaso.

Dino is nosy.

dolce come un agnello

softie, lit. soft as a lamb

Aurora sembra dolce come un agnello, ma quando si arrabbia, diventa una iena.

Aurora seems to be a softie, but when she gets upset, she's a beast.

buono, buona come il pane

sweet as pie, lit. as good as bread

Cecilia può essere buona come il pane. Dipende da come le parli.

Cecilia can be sweet as pie. It depends on how you speak to her.

non cagare qualcuno

to not give a shit about someone, lit. to not shit someone

Puoi fargli tutti i complimenti che vuoi, Cosimo non ti caga lo stesso.

You can compliment him all you want, Cosimo doesn't give a shit about you.

tamarro, m

redneck, usually from the country

Quel brutto tamarro si crede il più bello del mondo.

This ugly redneck thinks he's the best-looking in the world.

grezzo, grezza

brutish, rough around the edges

Emiliano è una brava persona anche se un po' grezzo.

Emiliano is a nice guy even if he's a bit rough around the edges.

scaccia fighe, m

nerd, lit. one who chases pussy away

Che scaccia fighe! Passi tutto il tempo libero davanti al computer.

What a nerd! You spend all your free time in front of the computer.

metterci la mano/mettere la mano sul fuoco

to swear/bet, lit. to put the hand there/on the fire

Fabrizio ci metterebbe la mano che la sua ragazza gli è fedele.

Fabrizio swears his girlfriend is faithful to him.

simpa, m, f

nice, abbr. of *simpatico*

Suo marito mi è sembrato molto simpa.

Her husband seemed very nice to me.

alterna, m, f

alternative person, abbr. of *alternativo*

Frequenta locali underground da quando esce con un'alterna.

He frequents underground clubs since he's been dating an alternative girl.

andare contro corrente

to be alternative, lit. to go against the stream

Da adolescente Mirco andava contro corrente ma adesso fa carriera militare.

When he was a teen, Mirco used to be alternative, but now he has a military career.

fare una figura di merda

to be ridiculous, lit. to make a shitty face

Hai fatto una figura di merda al suo matrimonio.

You were ridiculous at his wedding.

giocarsi la pelle

to risk one's skin, lit. to play one's skin

Guida tranquillamente; non giocarti la pelle per guadagnare qualche minuto.

Drive calmly; don't risk your skin to gain a few minutes.

dare una mano
to give a hand
Chi di voi mi dà una mano?
Who's willing to give me a hand?

mettersi nelle mani di qualcuno
to put oneself in someone's hands
Mettiti nelle mani del chirurgo—andrà tutto bene.
Put yourself in the surgeon's hands—it'll be all right.

fare il passo più lungo della gamba
out of one's league, lit. to make the pass longer than the leg
Fai il passo più lungo della gamba con questo progetto. Ti conviene aspettare.
This project is out of your league. You'd better wait.

avere la testa tra le nuvole
to have one's head in the clouds
Verso la fine dell'anno scolastico, tutti gli allievi hanno la testa tra nuvole.
At the end of the school year, all students have their heads in the clouds.

darsi arie
to put on airs
Non mi piacciono le ragazzine come te che si danno arie.
I don't like little girls like you that put on airs.

tirarsela
to show off, lit. to lead it to oneself
Leonardo ha la Vespa nuova e se la tira di brutto.
Leonardo has a new Vespa and is showing off like crazy.

pavoneggiarsi/mostrare i muscoli

to show off, lit. to act like a peacock/show the muscles

Paolo si pavoneggia davanti alle ragazze. Quanto è ridicolo!

Paolo is showing off in front of the girls. How ridiculous!

TOO UPTIGHT:

Most Italians pretend to be *alla buona*, "uncomplicated," and won't normally act like *principini*, "little princes," or *principessina*, "little princesses." Even during the competition of Miss Italia, all candidates present themselves as *la ragazza della porta accanto*, "the girl next door": all natural, genuine, and simple, the kind of person that would never participate in a beauty contest unless she was persuaded to do so. Italians don't like uptight people, whose strange attitude makes them look like *un cacasodo*, "someone who shits hard" or *ragazze che pensano di avere la figa d'oro*, "chicks who think they have a golden pussy." The way snobs keep their noses up makes them look "as if there was a bad smell in the air," *come se avessero la puzza sotto il naso*. This inability to act normally is explained by the expression *avere ingoiato il manico della scopa*, "to have a stick up one's ass."

gasato, gasata

excited, lit. fizzy

Angie è molto gasata perché oggi il suo ragazzo ritorna dagli Stati Uniti.

Angie is very excited because today her boyfriend is coming back from the United States.

pettegolo, pettegola

gossiper

Pettegola, hai detto tutto alla tua amica quando mi avevi promesso di tenerlo segreto.
You gossip, you told your friend everything when you promised to keep it a secret.

avere un buon naso per qualcosa
to have a good nose for something
Mark ha un buon naso per gli affari.
Mark has a good nose for business.

avere la testa dura/essere testardo
to be hard-headed
Quel marocchino ha la testa dura; gli ho detto che non mi serve niente, ma insiste.
That street merchant is hard-headed; I told him I didn't need any-thing, but he's insisting.

verme, m
worm
Sei un verme; non trovo le parole per quello che hai fatto.
You're a worm; I can't find the words for what you did.

avere le mani di pasta frolla
to be a butterfingers, lit. to have pastry hands
Ha spaccato tre bicchieri asciugando i piatti. Eliseo ha le mani di pasta frolla.
He broke three glasses while drying the dishes. Eliseo is a butterfingers.

CHAPTER EIGHTEEN

Amore mio:
Love is a Wonderful Thing

Even in beautiful Italian, love has its own language. As if this wasn't difficult enough, *l'amore* has its own colloquial expressions and slang that non-natives don't have a chance of understanding. Don't let your foreign romances get spoiled because of miscommunication—learn a few Dirty Italian words or phrases to excite your handsome *gondoliere* or gorgeous *gelataia*.

We can split the Italian male population in two main categories. One has a high level of testosterone and *machismo*, which can manifest itself in either chivalrous or egotistical behavior. The others, *i metrosessuale*, are anti-macho *per eccellenza*. They pay a lot of attention to their looks and may wear fancier underwear than you do. Their overdeveloped femininity can trick you into thinking they are harmless. Making the distinction would be easy if some machos didn't also dress up *all'ultima moda,* in the latest style.

If you are a female tourist and an easy target, you'll be the center of attention, and some men may even fight for you. You'll feel *importante* and will certainly spend a wonderful *notte* or two . . . Then another *turista* will come and your lover, *macho* or not, will leave you *per un'altra. È la vita.*

Now for the scoop on Italian ladies: *le ragazze italiane* are known as some of the most beautiful in Europe (a few years ago, before many Eastern European countries joined the EU, they were number one). *Gusto nel vestire* and Latin charm will give you *un torcicollo*, "a stiff neck," while walking in the streets. An *Italiana* doesn't just look great—her personality will surprise you. If jealousy is a sign of love, then be prepared to find the most intense love you can imagine. Meeting your future mother-in-law will give you a good idea of how your *tesoro* will look in a few years. If you don't want the princess you met to be transformed into a toad, then keep jealousy high. She'll do *tutto il necessario* to stay the cutie you first met.

First Sight

piacere una cifra/un casino
to really like, lit. to like a cipher/a brothel
Mi piace una cifra quando mi parli in francese.
I really like when you speak French to me.

cotto, cotta/stracotto, stracotta
in love, lit. cooked/overcooked
La mia ex è ancora cotta di me.
My ex is still in love with me.

avere/prendersi una cotta per qualcuno
to have a crush on someone, lit. to have/take oneself a cooking for someone
Ambrogio si è preso una cotta per Carla.
Ambrogio has a crush on Carla.

sbavare dietro a qualcuno/per qualcuno

to drool over someone

Davide sbavava per la ragazza del suo amico.

Davide was drooling over his friend's girlfriend.

innamorato, innamorata perso di qualcuno

head over heels for someone, lit. lost in love with someone

Al primo sguardo, Aldo si è innamorato perso di mia sorella.

At first sight, Aldo fell head over heels for my sister.

fare gli occhi dolci (a qualcuno)

to make doe eyes, lit. to make sweet eyes to someone

Quando Ornella ti fa gli occhi dolci non le puoi rifiutare niente.

When Ornella makes doe eyes, you can't refuse her anything.

pollastrella, f

chick

Guido ti presenterà qualche pollastrella.

Guido'll introduce you to some chicks.

principe azzurro, m

Prince Charming, lit. blue prince

Kristen aspetta ancora il principe azzurro.

Kristen is still waiting for Prince Charming.

pezzo di ghiaccio/ghiacciolo, m

ice queen, lit. piece of ice/popsicle

Non pensare neanche di chiedere aiuto a Leila; è un vero pezzo di ghiaccio.

Don't even think of asking Leila for help; she's an ice queen.

piccioncini, mpl

lovebirds, lit. little turtledoves

Quanto è carina questa vecchia coppia. Sembrano ancora due piccioncini.

This old couple is so cute. They still look like lovebirds.

farfallone, m

swinging single, lit. big butterfly

Sei un farfallone perché non hai ancora trovato quella giusta.

You're still a swinging single because you haven't met the right one yet.

anima gemella, f

soul mate, lit. twin soul

Andrea cerca l'anima gemella.

Andrea is looking for his soul mate.

Apprentice Lover

buttarsi

to have a go, lit. to throw oneself

Sono molto timido, ma mi butto lo stesso vado a chiederle di uscire con me.

I'm very shy, but I'll have a go at asking her out.

abbordare

to approach; from Navy jargon for attack

Bruno ha paura di abbordare ragazze nei locali.

Bruno is afraid to approach girls in pubs.

rimorchiare

to pick up a guy/girl, lit. to haul

Se ascolti bene Luciano, saprai tutti i segreti per rimorchiare le tipe più belle.

If you listen to Luciano well, you'll know all the tricks to pick up the prettiest girls.

fare il filo a qualcuno

to flirt, lit. to be very nice with someone

Paola ha fatto il filo a Olivia per sei mesi invano.

Paola has been flirting with Olivia for six months in vain.

provarci con qualcuno

to come on to someone, lit. to try with someone

Omar ci ha provato con Sue, ma lei non ci ha fatto caso.

Omar came on to Sue, but she didn't pay any attention.

farsi/non farsi vivo

to show up/not show up

Fatti vivo alle sette di mattina, sennò partiamo senza di te.

Show up at seven a.m., or else we leave without you.

tirare un pacco/bidone a qualcuno

to stand someone up, lit. to pull a pack/bucket to someone

Occhio a te se mi tiri un bidone domani sera.

You'll be sorry if you stand me up tomorrow evening.

piantare in asso qualcuno

to walk out on someone, lit. to plant someone in ace

Monica è uscita a cena con me, ma mentre ero in bagno, mi ha piantato in asso.

Monica went out to dinner with me, but when I was in the restroom, she walked out on me.

dare buca/il due di picche a qualcuno
to not show to a date, lit. to give hole /the two of spades
Come ha potuto darti buca, 'sta brutta stronza!
How dare she not show to your date, that bitch!

beccarsi un due di picche
to be rejected, lit. to get a two of spades
Tuo fratello si è beccato un due di picche da Costanza.
Your brother got rejected by Costanza.

Italy has two national card games, scopa *and* briscola.
In briscola, *the highest card is the ace and two is the lowest. In* scopa, *spades is a worthless suit and twos are bad cards. In both games, getting a two of spades destroys any hope of winning.*

essere l'ultima ruota del carro/il terzo incomodo
to be the third wheel, lit. to be the last wheel of the chariot/the uncomfortable third
Non voglio essere il terzo incomodo, ragazzi. È meglio se vi lascio da soli.
I don't want to be the third wheel, guys. It's better if I leave you alone.

reggere il moccolo/la candela
to be the third wheel, lit. to hold the candle
Franco ha dovuto reggere il moccolo ieri sera, ed è ancora arrabbiatissimo.
Franco had to be the third wheel last night, and he's still very upset.

Declarations of Love, Kissing, and Petting

TVB, TVTB

I like you, I like you a lot, acronym of *Ti Voglio Bene, Ti Voglio Tanto Bene*

Sui muri della chiesa, Giusi ha scritto in grande: Mirco, TVTB.

Giusi wrote in big letters on the church walls: Mirco, I like you a lot.

Italians have a tendency to use a lot of vezzeggiativi, *"sweet names," in relationships. You don't always need to be part of a couple though, to hear someone call you* gioia *"joy,"* bellezza *"beauty," or* tesoro, *but calling someone* biscotto, amore, amoruccio *"little love,"* ciccio, ciccia *"fat,"* micio, *or* micia *implies more intimacy.*

andare a braccetto

to walk arm in arm

Era bello, ma strano, vedere sua nonna a braccetto con un nuovo compagno.

It was nice, but strange, to see her grandmother walking arm in arm with a new companion.

limonare/fare dei limoni

to make out; from *limone*, lemon (squeezing the breasts like lemons)

Pino ha preso la sua ragazza per mano e sono andati a limonare sulla spiaggia.
Pino took his girlfriend by the hand and they went to make out on the beach.

baciare con la lingua
to French kiss, lit. to kiss with the tongue
Baciami per davvero, baciami con la lingua!
Kiss me for real, French kiss me!

DAMMI UN BACIO!
The French kiss, *il bacio alla francese*, comes from France. The tongue activity inspired *slinguare*, a new verb built on *lingua*. *Baciare con la lingua*, "to kiss with the tongue," is less vulgar and less trendy at the same time. *Sbaciucchiare* is a regional form of *baciare*. *La slinguata*, *lo sbaciucchiamento* and *il bacio con la lingua* are the Italian translations of "the French kiss." While France is just next door, the authors highly recommend you try it out on this side of the border.

succhiotto, m (dialect)
hickey; from *succhiare*, to suck
Sue ha notato il succhiotto sul collo di suo marito e ha fatto una scenata.
Sue noticed the hickey on her husband's neck and made a scene.

cercare le coccole
to ask for tickles (to be touched), lit. to look for tickles
Enzo ha cercato le coccole ma la sua ragazza non aveva tempo per lui.
Enzo asked for tickles but his girlfriend had no time for him.

For Better or for Worse

accasarsi
to get married, shacked up; from *casa*, house, to put oneself in a house
Dopo anni di celibato, Giulio si è accasato con una ragazza per bene.
After years of being single, Giulio shacked up with a nice girl.

addio al celibato/nubilato, m
bachelor/bachelorette party, lit. bye to celibacy
Festeggeremo il tuo addio al nubilato nel nostro locale preferito.
We'll celebrate your bachelorette party in our favorite nightclub.

scappatella extraconiugale, f
affair, lit. extraconjugal escape
In tutti questi anni di matrimonio, nessuno di loro ha fatto una scappatella extraconiugale.
In all their years of marriage, not one of them has had an affair.

fare le corna a qualcuno
to cheat on someone, lit. to make horns
Patrice non aveva mai fatto le corna a sua moglie prima di incontrare Raven.
Patrice had never cheated on his wife before he met Raven.

mollare qualcuno
to dump/ditch someone, lit. to release
Maria ha mollato il suo ragazzo quando ha realizzato che l'aveva tradita.
Maria dumped her boyfriend when she realized that he had cheated on her.

TIME TO SPLIT:

As you've heard, Italian lovers are jealous, possessive, or macho. As a consequence, it's sometimes harder to end a relationship than to start a new one. The Italians either can't or don't want to understand it's over. It may be because your words weren't the ones they wanted to hear. Building a repertoire of some helpful break-up expressions can ease this difficulty. *Ho chiuso con te*, literally "I'm closed with you" or *la nostra storia è chiusa*, "our story is closed," makes your intentions quite clear. *Facciamola finita*, "let's finish it," and *diamoci un taglio*, literally "let's give it a cut," are invitations to end the relationship mutually. To send someone packing speaks of travel with no return—this same idea in Italian is present in *mandare qualcuno a quel paese*, literally "to send someone to that town." Finally, *scaricare qualcuno*, lit. "to offload someone," is the closest translation of "to dump someone."

tornare con qualcuno/assieme/insieme a qualcuno
to get back together with someone
Toby, sono sicuro che tornerai con Simona molto presto. Siete due anime gemelle.
Toby, I'm sure that you and Simona will get back together soon. You two are soul mates.

CHAPTER NINETEEN

Voglia di sesso:

Partners and Their Private Parts

In order to make the most of your time in Italy, you'll need to know the basics when it comes to sex. This *capitolo* gives you a first look into various body parts and pleasures. Like a puzzle, you just have to make them fit. We're sure you can manage it . . .

While we'd have to write hundreds of pages to list every slang word in the domain of sex, here are a simple few to get you started. After all, knowing even one word is the first step. For those who want to know more than just parts of the body, we also provide you different personality types from the *casa chiesa oratorio* to the *scopamica*, and from *il segaiolo* to the *gigolo*.

Dick

No need to use a lot of imagination to understand these words. They all share a special shape and a hard aspect. Children will be told they have a *pisello*, "a pea," and that they shouldn't play with it in public. Dicks can take every form in slang, and what greater pleasure than mixing the two Italian main passions, sex and food? Would you like to eat some *piselli*, or *pisellini*, "peas" or "small peas"? Maybe the main course will be *una banana*, *il frutto dell'amore*, "the fruit of love." Animals play their part in inspiring these words. *L'uccello* and *l'uccello Padulo* (*che vola all'altezza del buco del culo*), "the bird" and "the bird called Padulo (that flies at the height of the asshole)" are common expressions. Comparisons with powerful, aggressive, or simply dangerous weapons and tools are often made. Careful, you may be beaten by a *dardo*, "bee stinger"! Don't fear to be beaten when receiving *colpi di manganello*, "baton hits"—it's just sex. Some do-it-yourself fans will recognize their favorite tools, such as *il trapano*, "the drill," or *il cacciavite*, "the screwdriver." Pretentious people will compare their dick with a *biga*, a tool used to lift heavy weights. Musicians will ask you to play their *tromba*, or if you can, *suonare il flauto di pelle*, "play the skin flute." And please, don't think you're going to see better in the dark while asked to hold *una candela*.

cappella, f
head of the dick, lit. chapel
Fammi succhiare la tua cappella.
Let me suck your dick.

Cappella *comes from* cappa. *Martin de Tours, a bishop, cut his cap in two pieces to give half of it to a beggar that crossed his way. Impressed by this act of generosity, his followers kept the second half as a precious relic. The building around it was then called* cappella, *chapel. In a sign of respect to this glorious past, we'd appreciate if you go down on your knees . . .*

cazzo, m
dick
A giudicare dalla gobba al jeans, Renato deve avere un cazzo enorme.
Judging from the bulge in his jeans, Renato must have a big dick.

Keeping in mind the actual meaning, "dick," and also the predominance of the macho system, it is natural that you'll find cazzi *everywhere.* Che cazzo fai?, *"What the f**k are you doing?"* non c'era un cazzo da fare, *"there wasn't anything to do,"* sto cazzo di motore, *"that bloody engine,"* and Cazzo! Ho mancato il treno, *"F**k! I missed the train." Anywhere you travel, you'll be sure to meet a bunch of* teste di cazzo, *"dickheads." Did you know Italians associate their dick with superstitious powers? If* un'ambulanza *or* un carro funebre *crosses their way, males will squeeze their balls with one hand while pointing the index and the pinkie of the other to the floor, drawing some kind of horns, to protect them from* la sfiga.

palle, balle, fpl
balls
Non venirmi sopra, ciccia. Ho paura che mi schiacci le palle.
Don't get on top of me, sweetie. I'm scared you'll squish my balls.

coglione, m
testicle; from the Latin *coleus*, testicle
Ho tirato un calcio nei coglioni a mio fratello.
I kicked my brother in the balls.

Pussy

bernarda, f (Nord)
pussy, lit. feminine form of Bernardo
Se ti mostro il mio pene mi fai vedere la bernarda?
If I show you my dick, will you show me your pussy?

fregna (Roma)/mona (Veneto)
pussy
Raga'! Ieri Tania m'ha fatto vede' la mona!
Guys! Yesterday Tania showed me her pussy!

fessa, f (Sud)/ ferita, f
cunt, lit. fissure/wound
La spogliarellista spalancava le gambe per mostrare la fessa al pubblico.
The stripper spread her legs to show her cunt to the crowd.

L'ORIGINE DEL MONDO:
The fruit of sin for certain fanatics, *la figa*, "fig," is by far the most popular slang term for "pussy." Sharing their sweetness, their juiciness, or maybe simply their shape, the following words should inspire a delicious *macedonia*, fruit salad. Would you like to snack on an *albicocca*, "apricot"? Or maybe you'll prefer a *susina* or *prugna*, "prune"? If you don't like fruit, what about a *lecca-lecca*, "lollypop," then? In any case, in Italy you're certain to find something sweet. To explain the sexual difference between boys and girls, Italian parents use terms such as *patata*, *patatina*, "potato"; *fragola*, *fragolina*, "strawberry"; *farfalla*, *farfallina*, "butterfly"; and *passera*, *passerina*, "sparrow." These vegetables and animals lead to other interesting comparisons. Once the ice is broken or completely melted, your Italian beauty may ask you, *Leccami la*

lumaca, la topa; or *la sorca, la gatta,* or *la ferita.* What kind of a freak would ask you to lick a snail, mouse, cat, or wound? Still don't get it? Spit out the snail, stop torturing the poor pets, and do what you were kindly asked to do.

coso,cosa/cosino, cosina

dick/pussy, lit. thing/little thing

Non parlare della cosina quando c'è Hilary; la metti in imbarazzo.

Don't speak about pussy when Hilary is around; it embarrasses her.

Accessories

cappuccio, m

condom, foreskin, lit. hood

La sua ragazza americana non aveva mai visto un cazzo con il cappuccio.

His American girlfriend had never seen a dick with a foreskin.

guanto, m

condom, lit. glove

Non vorrai mica metterla incinta la prima notte? Metti un guanto!

You don't really want to get her pregnant the first night, do you? Put on a condom!

CONDOMS:

The Italian birth rate is the lowest in Europe. Birth control methods, especially condoms, are widely used. War against STDs or MST has been declared. Soldiers go to the front with "bullet-proof vest," *un antiproiettile,* and parachutists will never forget *il loro paracadute*. In order to keep healthy, you wouldn't go out without a *vestitino*, or forget to wear *i guanti*, "gloves," if you were a surgeon, would you? But the main slang term for condom is still *Goldone*. The trade name of this popular Italian condom was inspired from the condom brought by American GI's during World War II, the gold one. The guys didn't only free Italy from fascists, but also women's libido from motherhood.

grilletto, m
clit, lit. little cricket
Ha un grilletto enorme, impossibile sbagliarsi.
She has a huge clit, impossible to miss it.

cespuglio, m/aiola, f
pubic hair, lit. bush/fence made with bushes
Se ti rasi il cespuglio, ti lecco la figa, tesoro.
If you shave your pubic hair, I'll lick your pussy, sweetie.

pornazzo/porno/filmaccio, m
porn movie, lit. dirty movie
Selen ha girato in parecchi filmacci amatoriali per pagarsi gli studi.
Selen acted in several amateur porn movies to pay for her studies.

Friends

casa-chiesa-oratorio
goody two-shoes, lit. house-church-parish youth club
Adriano era tutto casa-chiesa-oratorio prima di incontrare Stefania.
Adriano was a goody two-shoes before he met Stefania.

zitella, zitellona, f

old maid

Deciditi ad uscire con un ragazzo o finirai zitellona!

Decide to go out with a guy or you'll end up as an old maid!

avere la figa di legno/d'oro, f

to think one's shit doesn't stink, lit. to have a wooden/golden pussy

Pensa di avere la figa d'oro?

Does she think her shit doesn't stink?

guardone, m

voyeur, lit. big looker

Smettila di fare il guardone—girati mentre mi spoglio.

Stop being a voyeur—turn while I'm undressing.

marpione, m

guy who tries every girl, lit. pubic lice

Ivo è un marpione ma si becca solo due di picche.

Ivo tries every girl but he's constantly rejected.

segaiolo, m

jerk-off; from *sega*, saw

Dice che suo marito è una bestia a letto. A mio parere è solo un segaiolo.

She says her husband is a god in bed. I think he's just a jerk-off.

travesto, m

transvestite, abbr. of *travestito*

Da quando Claudio è diventato travesto, i suoi genitori non gli parlano più.

Since Claudio has become a transvestite, his parents don't speak to him anymore.

GAYS:

Culo, *culone*, *culattina*, and *culatone*, come from the part of the body associated with the gay community, the ass. The ear, *orecchio*, is another part of the body supposedly involved in gay sex, as it seems to be the only part of the face that can be kissed during lovemaking without risking *un torcicollo*, "a sore neck." As a result, gays are known as *orecchione*, *rechione*, and *ricchione*. Male homosexuals are not considered men. Machos call them *effe*, *effeminato*, "effeminate"; *zia*, "aunt"; or *femminuccia*, "little female." *Frocio*, *finocchio*, "fennel" and *checca*, from *chicco*, are the most popular and derogative terms, the equivalents of "queer" or "fag."

nave scuola, f

Mrs Robinson, lit. school boat

Betty fa la nave scuola perchè preferisce gli amanti giovani.

Betty plays the Mrs Robinson because she prefers young lovers.

divoratrice d'uomini, f

man-eater

Camilla è una divoratrice d'uomini.

Camilla is a man-eater.

stracciamanici, f

insatiable girl, lit. who rips sticks (dicks)

Ho passato la notte con una stracciamanici. Sono esausto.

I spent the night with an insatiable girl. I'm exhausted.

SLUT:

What does a religious, conservative community call a horny woman? Comparisons to the animal world abound: *pantera*, "man-eater," from "panther"; *allupata*, "horny," from *lupo*, "wolf"; and *assatanata*, "horny" from *Satana*, "Satan." This lack of reserve is also compared to hunger. Women are described as *affamate*, *golose*, *golosone*, *vogliose*, *arrapate*, "hungry" or "starving"—that is, "sexually aroused" or "excited."

cagnaccio, cagnaccia

slut, lit. dirty bitch; from *cagna*, bitch

Se mi lasci, dirò a tutti che sei una cagnaccia.

If you leave me, I'll tell everyone you're a slut.

putanella, f

easy, slut, lit. little whore

Che putanella Lola! Dà il suo numero di cellulare ad ogni ragazzo figo.

Lola is such a slut! She gives her cell phone number to every cute guy.

rimorchiatore, m

seducer, lit. tug boat

Fausto é un gran rimorchiatore: ogni sera una diversa.

Fausto is a big seducer: every night another girl.

sventrapapere, m

womanizer, lit. one who guts goslings

Hai lasciato tua figlia uscire con quello sventrapapere? Vuoi diventare nonna?

You let your daughter go out with that womanizer? Do you want to become a grandmother?

conquistatore/dongiovanni/donnaiolo, m

womanizer, lit. conqueror/Don Giovanni/ladies-man

Non avrei mai pensato che Salvatore fosse un donnaiolo.

I would never have thought Salvatore was a womanizer.

gigolò, m

gigolo

Qualche clandestino fa il gigolò per stare in Italia.

Some illegals play the gigolo to stay in Italy.

sporcaccione, sporcacciona

pervert, lit. big dirty one

Sei proprio una sporcacciona, ma mi piaci lo stesso.

You're such a pervert, but I like you anyway.

porco, porca/porcello, porcella/ porcellone, porcellona

pig, pervert, lit. pig/little pig/big pig

Maddalena è una vera porca; vuole finire la serata a letto con due tipi.

Maddalena is such a pervert; she wants to end the night in bed with two guys.

scopabile

f**kable, lit. sweepable

Niente male la tua suocera; anzi direi che è proprio scopabile.

Your mother in law is not so bad looking; in fact I would say she's quite f**kable.

Interesting words have been invented to say a person is not so bad, and that one would consider f**king. The image of the well-lubed piston going up and down

brought about the adjective pistonabile. Pisello *is slang for "penis" and* pisellabile *comes from it. Some comfort is added with* materassabile, *"that which can be put on a mattress." Finally* (in)chiavabile, *from* chiavare, *to have sex, is to have sex inspired by keys, locks, and their magic combination.*

scopatore, scopatrice
someone who is f**king, lit. sweeper
Nel motel si sentivano bene gli scopatori della porta accanto.
In the motel we could hear the people f**king next door.

scopamico, scopamica
f**kfriend; from *scopare*, f**k, and *amico*, friend
Sola in casa e un po' depressa, Francesca decise di chiamare il suo scopamico.
Alone in her house and a bit depressed, Francesca decided to call her f**kfriend.

avere una bocca da bocchinara
to have dicksucking lips; from *bocca*, mouth
Roberta si è offesa quando le ho detto che aveva una bocca da bocchinara.
Roberta got upset when I told her she had dicksucking lips.

leccacazzi/succhiacazzi, m, f
dicklicker/dicksucker
Anna è la migliore leccacazzi del paese.
Anna is the best dicksucker in town.

CHAPTER TWENTY

Obbiettivo sesso:

Dirty, Dirtier, and Dirtiest Italian

Did you come straight to this chapter? You may have very little paid vacation per year and the intention to make it worth its while in Italy is understandable. Learn the following words and pay attention to them in conversation. They may be addressed to you! Don't ruin your chances though, and be sure to take advantage of every possible opportunity . . . it may take years before you save enough money to come back to Italy.

If you read the previous chapters patiently, then your *pazienza* will come to an end soon. *Talk Dirty Italian* promised to teach you to talk dirty, and the final step is very near. But remember, what's the point of talking dirty if you still use expressions like "I'd like to have sexual intercourse with you"? This chapter is meant to bridge that gap, or *colmare quel vuoto*. In the past few chapters we have explored the dark side of Italian, and now it's time to know what dirty things they can do with their tongues and how they say those dirty things in their mother tongue. Happy reading.

Physiological Reactions

venire duro/dritto

to get a hard-on, lit. to get hard/straight

Ogni volta che ti vedo in bikini, mi viene duro.

Every time I see you in a bikini, I get a hard-on.

bagnarsi

to get wet, lit. to wet oneself

Azzurra si è bagnata tutta quando le ho rivelato le mie fantasie.

Azzurra got wet when I revealed my fantasies to her.

brodo, m/sborra, f

cum, lit. broth; from *sborrare*, to come out

Le lenzuola della camera d'albergo erano macchiate di sborra.

The sheets of the hotel room were stained with cum.

drizzarsi

to get hard, lit. to become straight

Il suo cazzo non si drizza quando lo tocco.

His dick doesn't get hard when I touch it.

sborrata, f

cum shot; from *sborrare*

Carlotta si è presa una sborrata in faccia.

XXX: Too dirty to translate

sborrare/sbrodare

to come, lit. to come out; from *brodo*, broth

Filippo sborra dopo due minute di sesso.

XXX: Too dirty to translate

venire

to come

Che cattivo; l'hai tirato fuori quando stavo per venire.

You're a meany; you pulled out when I was about to come!

Warming Up

ditale/ditalino, m

masturbation; from *dito*, finger, only for women

Milena mi guardava negli occhi mentre si faceva un ditalino.

Milena was looking at me while she fingered herself.

toccarsi

to masturbate, lit. to touch oneself

Sono sicuro che qualcuno di voi si toccherà quando leggerà quel capitolo.

I'm sure some of you will touch yourselves when reading this chapter.

sega, f

wank, lit. saw

Viviana sa fare delle belle seghe.

Viviana gives a good wank.

farsi una sega/un raspone/una pipa (pippa)

to jerk off, lit. to make oneself a saw/polish/pipe

Dovresti farti una pipa più spesso, Gigi, sei troppo nervoso.

You should jerk off more often, Gigi, you're too nervous.

pugnetta, f

handjob, lit. little fist

Mario si fa le pugnette di nascosto in classe!
Mario gives himself handjobs during lessons!

(sega) spagnola, f

titty f**k, lit. Spanish (saw)
Che tettona, la tua tipa. Deve fare delle ottime spagnole.
What huge titties your chick has. She must make a wonderful titty f**k.

Oral Sex

andare di bocca

to give head, lit. to go with the mouth
Tracey va di bocca appena apri i pantaloni. È una vera porca.
Tracey gives head as soon as one opens his pants. She's such a slut.

bocchino/pompino, m

blowjob, lit. mouthful; from *pompare*, to pump
Sono alle stelle quando mi fai un bocchino.
I'm on cloud nine when you give me a blowjob.

ciucciare/succhiare il cazzo

to suck dick; *ciucciare* is a childish term for *succhiare*
Sappiamo tutti quanto ti piace ciucciare il cazzo.
We all know how much you like to suck dicks.

pompare qualcuno

to suck, lit. to pump someone
Pompami più forte, sto per venire.
Suck me harder, I'm about to come.

suonare il flauto di/in pelle

to give a blowjob, lit. to play the skin flute

A scuola Lili non è dotata per niente, ma non conosco nessuno che suoni il flauto di pelle come lei.

At school Lili is not talented at all, but I don't know anyone who can give a blowjob like she does.

leccare la cosina/leccarla (a qualcuno)

to eat someone's pussy, lit. to lick the little thing/to lick it to someone

Federica, lasciami leccare la cosina. Vedrai che ti piacerà.

Federica, let me eat your pussy. You'll see that you'll like it.

brucare il cespuglio, f

to eat bush lit. to feed on bush

Tatiana bruca il cespuglio di Elena.

Tatiana is eating Elena's bush.

Sex

andare in camporella/imboscarsi

to have sex outside, lit. to go to the little field/to hide in the wood

Giorgio e Cristina hanno preso la macchina per andare in camporella.

Giorgio and Cristina took the car to have sex outside.

imboscarsi

to hide (in order to have sex), lit. to hide in the woods

Lara e Fabio si sono imboscati in macchina ma la polizia li ha beccati.

Lara and Fabio hid in the car to have sex but the policeman caught them.

sverginare

to deflower, lit. to devirginize

Jonathan cerca una pollastrella da sverginare.

Jonathan is looking for a chick to deflower.

fare sesso

to have sex

Non posso più aspettare, devo fare sesso stasera!

I can't wait anymore; I have to have sex tonight!

farsi qualcuno

to do someone, lit. to do oneself someone

Stasera Franco vuole farsi una ragazza ad ogni costo. Non l'ho mai visto così eccitato.

Tonight Franco really wants to do a girl. I've never seen him so horny.

fottere

to f**k

Vai a farti fottere, troia!

Go f**k yourself, slut!

Lit. Go get f**ked, sow!

portarsi qualcuno a letto

to bring someone to bed

Il mio compagno di camera si porta a letto ogni sera una ragazza diversa.

Every night my roommate brings another girl to bed.

mettere

to do, lit. to put

Elisa mi ha detto che se volevo metterla, potevo chiamarla a qualunque ora.
Elisa told me if I wanted to do her, I could call her anytime.

metterlo dentro (a qualcuno)

to do (someone), lit. to put it inside (someone)
Stai zitto, non dire niente. Mettimelo dentro.
Shush, don't speak anymore. Just do me.

scopare

to f**k, lit. to sweep
Basta con le chiacchiere, è tempo di scopare!
Enough speaking now, let's f**k.

ciulare (Nord)

to f**k; from *ciula*, dick
Samuele era così eccitato che avrebbe ciulato qualsiasi ragazza con la minigonna.
Samuele was so horny that he would have f**ked any girl with a miniskirt.

scopata, f

f**k; from *scopa*, broom
Mi piacerebbe una bella scopata con quelle ragaza cubo.
I'd like a good f**k with that go-go dancer.

trombare qualcuno

to f**k; from *tromba*, trumpet
Una figa come tua sorella me la tromberei con piacere.
I'd like to f**k a hottie like your sister.

scopare a pecorina

to f**k doggy-style, lit. sheep-f**king

Alessandro scopa solo a pecorina.
Alessandro only f**ks doggy-style.

VUOI FOTTERE?

There are fewer ways to make love than ways to say it, and everyone has his specialty and preferences. For whom sex is a question of strength and power, as well as for DIY addicts, *impalare*, "to impale," and *trapanare*, "to drill," are the preferred synonyms. The analogy of key and keyhole for dick and pussy inspired the verb *chiavare* as another way of saying "to f**k" and the word *una chiavata* as "a f**k." Greedy guys will try to *inzuppare il biscotto*, "to dip the cookie." Sportive women will *cavalcare* their Italian *stallone* and musicians will find double pleasure *trombando*, "trumpeting." You may be surprised when you realize that *andare a farsi un giro in giostra* wasn't an invitation for a ride on the merry-go-round with some Italian, but indeed an invitation to have sex. Most Italians prefer *scopare* to working . . . and to think there are still people pretending housecleaning is a bore!

cosina veloce/sveltina, f
quickie, lit. fast little thing; from *svelto*, fast
Ti andrebbe una sveltina in macchina?
Would you mind a quickie in the car?

sbrodolata, f
quickie; from *brodo*, broth
Karen e il suo amoroso hanno fatto una sbrodolata nel parco pubblico.
Karen and her lover had a quickie in the public park.

ammucchiata, f
orgy; from *ammucchiare*, to pile

La serata è finita in un'ammucchiata.

The party ended in an orgy.

darla (via)

to give it up, lit. to give it (away)

Nelly è la ragazza più popolare del liceo perché la dà via subito.

Nelly is the most popular girl in high school because she gives it up right away.

Anal

buggerare

to f**k in the ass; from the English, to bugger

Annamaria si è fatta buggerare ieri ed oggi stenta a camminare.

XXX: Too dirty to translate

ficcare qualcosa in culo a qualcuno

to shove something up someone's ass

Se non la pianti, te lo ficco in culo.

XXX: Too dirty to translate

prenderlo/pigliarlo nel culo

to take it in the ass

Sabrina non vuole prenderlo nel culo da nessuno.

XXX: Too dirty to translate

BIBLIOGRAPHY

Burke, David. *Street Italian 1: The Best of Italian Slang*. (Hoboken, New Jersey: Wiley, 2000).

Chevalier, Bernard A. and Macagno, Gilles. *In bocca al lupo–Dans la gueule du loup: Mille et une expression et façon de dire pour apprendre l'italien*. (Paris, France: Ellipses Marketing, 2006).

De Mauro, Tullio. *Dizionario della lingua italiana* (Milan, Italy: Paravia, 2000).

Euvino, Gabrielle. *Dirty Italian: Everyday Slang from "What's Up?" to "F*ck Off!"* (Berkeley, California: Ulysses Press, 2006).

Delicio, Roland. *Merda!: The Real Italian You Were Never Taught in School*. (New York, New York: Plume,1993).

Gobetti, Daniela. *Italian Slang and Colloquial Expressions*. (Hauppauge, New York: Barron's Educational Series, 1999).

www.alternative-dictionaries.net/dictionary/Italian/

www.beginningwithi.com/italy/lang/itslanga.html

www.demauroparavia.it

http://digilander.libero.it/luirig/sinonimi/

www.dimensioni.org/articolo2_gennaio04.html#top

http://en.wikiquote.org/wiki/Italian_proverbs

http://espresso.repubblica.it/dettaglio-archivio/400221

http://italian.about.com

www.manuscritto.it

www.notam02.no/~hcholm/altlang/ht/Italian.html

www.scudit.net

www.slangypeople.com

www.wordreference.com